Summer Activities for the Gifted Student

Written by **Christy Yaros and Eliza Berkowi**

Illustrations by **Jannie Ho**

An imprint of Sterling Children's Books

FLASH KIDS, STERLING, and the distinctive STERLING logo are registered trademarks of Sterling Publishing Co., Inc.

Published by Sterling Publishing Co., Inc.
387 Park Avenue South, New York, NY 10016
Text and illustrations © 2010 by Flash Kids
Distributed in Canada by Sterling Publishing
c/o Canadian Manda Group, 165 Dufferin Street
Toronto, Ontario, Canada M6K 3H6
Distributed in the United Kingdom by GMC Distribution Services
Castle Place, 166 High Street, Lewes, East Sussex, England BN7 1XU
Distributed in Australia by Capricorn Link (Australia) Pty. Ltd.
P.O. Box 704, Windsor, NSW 2756, Australia

Cover image © Sean Justice/Corbis
Cover design and production by Mada Design, Inc.

Sterling ISBN 978-1-4114-2765-5

Manufactured in Canada

Lot #:
2   4   6   8   10   9   7   5   3   1
03/10

For information about custom editions, special sales, premium and
corporate purchases, please contact Sterling Special Sales
Department at 800-805-5489 or specialsales@sterlingpublishing.com.

Learning doesn't have to stop when the school year ends. Summer Activities for the Gifted Student offers thought-provoking exercises designed to challenge advanced learners during the vacation months. It reviews familiar skills and introduces new ones, all the while providing your child with the intellectual stimulation gifted children crave.

This workbook provides activities that challenge your child's unique abilities in all subject areas—language arts, math, social studies, and science. All materials presented here are carefully calibrated to match the average reading level, analytical capability, and subject interest of a gifted fifth grader. Reading passages present new vocabulary, math problems encourage critical-thinking skills, and writing exercises promote creativity. Science and social studies activities introduce new concepts while testing logic and problem-solving skills.

A few activities in this book will require finding additional information using outside sources such as an encyclopedia, a dictionary, or the Internet. Helping your child complete these exercises provides an opportunity to teach valuable research skills. In fact, all of the activities in this book provide a chance to work with your child to offer advice, guidance, praise, and encouragement. Have a wonderful summer and, most of all, have fun learning with your child!

Billy's Books

Billy's cat knocked all of the books off the bookshelf. Help Billy clean up his room by putting each book back on the shelf where it belongs. Round the numbers on the books to the nearest whole number, then draw a line to match each book to its corresponding shelf.

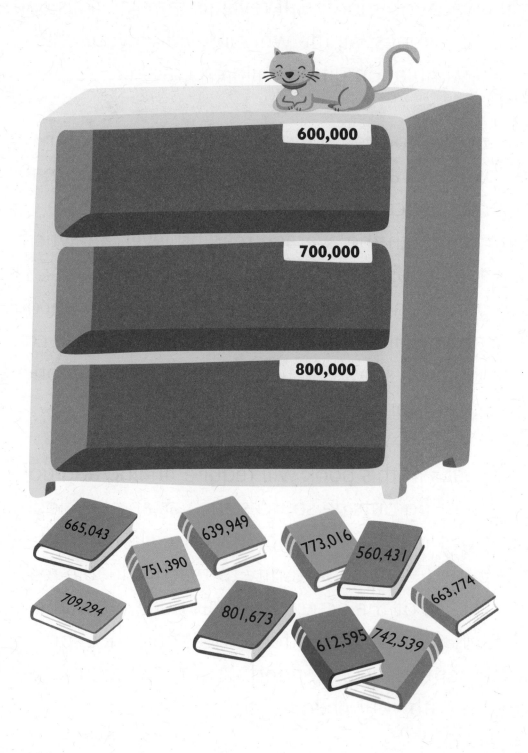

Slippery Synonyms

Mrs. Pearson was going to do a lesson today on synonyms, but she dropped all her notes. To help the teacher organize her lesson, draw lines to match the words that are synonyms.

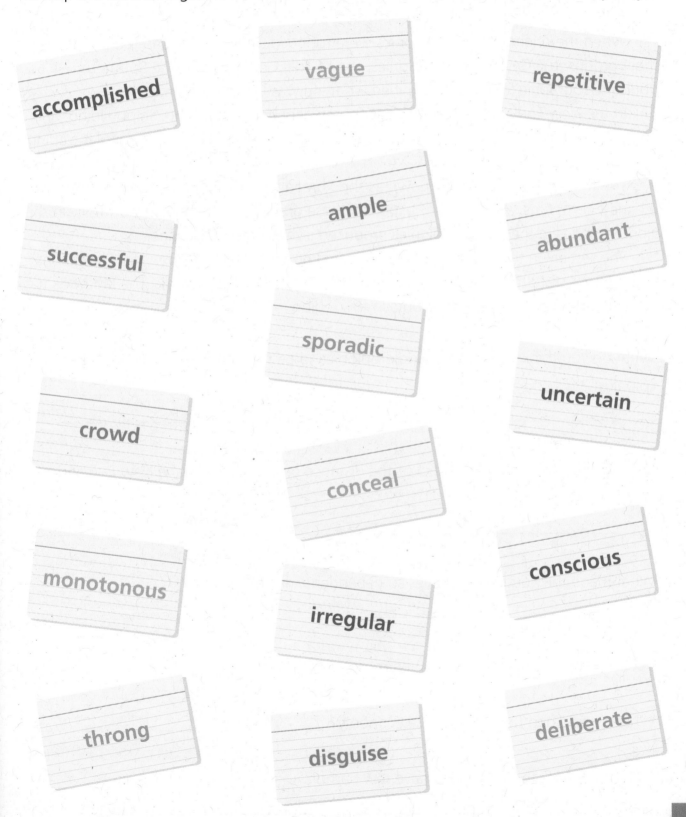

accomplished

vague

repetitive

ample

abundant

successful

sporadic

uncertain

crowd

conceal

conscious

monotonous

irregular

throng

disguise

deliberate

Colonial America

A **cause** is why something happens. An **effect** is what happens as a result of the cause.
Read the passage, then answer the questions below.

When the original thirteen colonies were founded, they were separated into three distinct groups: the New England Colonies, the Middle Colonies, and the Southern Colonies. Geographic features determined what life was like in each area.

In the New England Colonies, the economy depended on fishing, shipbuilding, and trading. This region was located near the ocean, and Boston Harbor was a popular trading port.

The Middle Colonies were known as the "breadbasket colonies." They grew crops like barley, corn, oats, and rye. They exported these grains, which grew so plentifully in this region. Factories in the Middle Colonies produced iron, textiles, and paper.

The settlers in the Southern Colonies were known for their plantations. Plantations are large areas of farmland where a family and its servants live and work. The land was flat, with fertile soil. There were few harbors in this region.

1. What do you think caused the Middle Colonies to be nicknamed the "breadbasket colonies"?_____

_____

2. What do you think was the effect of the distance of the ocean on the New England Colonies? _____

_____

3. What made the Southern Colonies so dependent on agriculture? _____

_____

4. In what region would a fisherman be most likely to settle? _____

5. Which region had the most diverse economy? _____

6. Why did the Southern Colonies have few harbors? _____

_____

Fantasy Fans

Melinda and her friends each claim to be the biggest fan of fantasy books. Complete the chart to discover what percent of each child's collection is fantasy books. The child with the largest percentage of fantasy books is the biggest fantasy fan! Round each answer to the nearest tenth.

Name	Total number of books	Number of fantasy books	Percentage of fantasy books
Melinda	109	33	
Carl	39	14	
Adrienne	97	27	
Tru	17	9	
Debbie	92	44	
Joey	55	24	
Wendy	116	49	
Ramon	87	17	
Marco	145	41	
Christina	73	38	

Who has the highest percentage of fantasy books in his or her collection? _____

The First Day of School

Read the story below. Each underlined word has an antonym in the word bank.
Find the matching antonyms and write them on the lines below.

> decrease   thanklessness   generous   optional
>
> admiration   revolutionary   flexible   remarkable

On the first day of fifth grade, Micah woke up ready to start a new school year. He went to his closet and pulled out his favorite pair of worn jeans and a sweatshirt with a hole in the elbow. When he went downstairs for breakfast, he was met with 1. disapproval from his mother. "You can't wear that on the first day of school! Looking nice is 2. necessary to make a good first impression!" she explained. Micah showed his 3. gratitude for his mother's advice by running back to his room to find a more suitable outfit. After briefly rummaging through his closet, he declared all of his clothes too 4. ordinary to make a good first impression at school. He needed to borrow something from his brother, Max.

"Max!" he yelled to his brother's room next door. "I need to borrow something nice to wear to school today!" Max sauntered into Micah's room with a frown on his face. "I don't think I want to lend you my nice clothes," Max said. "You don't take good care of your own clothes. See!" Max pointed to the hole in Micah's sweatshirt. "Come on, don't be 5. stubborn. I'll give you five dollars," Micah offered. Max thought for a moment, then said, "6. Multiply that by three. Then I'll let you borrow whatever you want." Micah laughed and said, "No way! You are so 7. stingy! I'll figure this out on my own."

Micah went back to his closet and pulled out the suit he wore to his cousin's wedding. It may not be the most 8. conventional outfit to wear to school, but at least I'll make a good impression, Micah thought!

1. _____

2. _____

3. _____

4. _____

5. _____

6. _____

7. _____

8. _____

Solar System Word Search

There are 15 words related to our solar system in the word search below. Find and circle the words.
Then write them on the lines as you find them.

```
                        X  I
                        Y  F
                     C  T  E  V
                     L  I  B  Y
                  E  M  V  W  A  L
                  L  A  A  Q  Q  X
Z  T  M  P  A  K  Z  K  R  R  Z  J  X  T  P  L  A  N  E  T
L  S  U  N  E  V  L  U  S  G  T  W  J  E  N  U  T  P  E  N
A  X  N  R  U  T  A  S  C  I  H  F  Q  R  Q  H  I  N
K  X  C  E  T  I  L  L  E  T  A  S  P  U  J  G
   W  J  K  W  R  C  M  A  C  U  F  W  Y  F
      F  X  V  Z  V  A  N  S  S  R  Q  P
      K  C  M  E  D  Q  O  S  J  T  O  A  J  J
         I  Q  T  E  M  O  C  H  M  U  E  N  U
         E  X  D  P  S  M  I  E  Z  D  T  P  R  N  U  S
         A  J  C  U  C  H  K        K  U  F  I  O  A  S
      Y  R  U  C  R  E  M           O  X  T  T  I  G  X
      P  W  T  V  E                    L  N  E  D  U
C  Z  U  Q                                F  R  Q  S
H  T                                      J  S
```

_____

_____   _____

_____   _____

_____   _____

_____   _____

_____   _____

_____   _____

Hexagonal Fill-In

Using the fractions in the figure below, determine the number that each fraction is multiplied by to get the next fraction. Going clockwise, fill in the empty boxes to complete each hexagon.

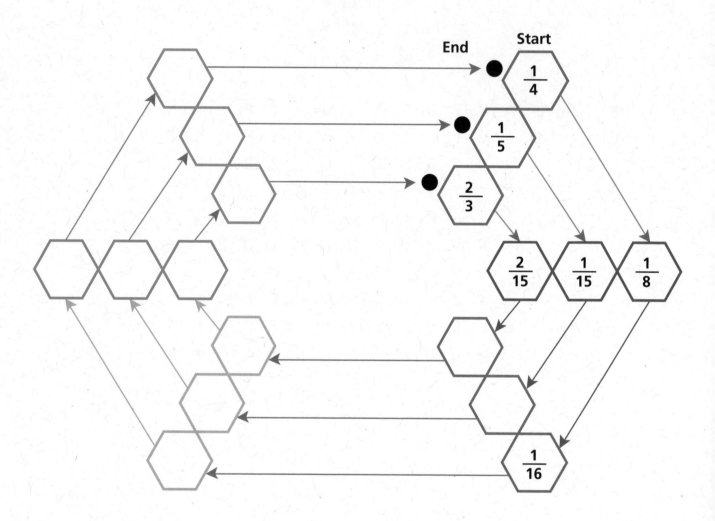

Izzy's Idioms

Izzy loves to speak in idioms. An **idiom** is a phrase that means something different from what the individual words mean. Larry is new in school, and Izzy is giving him some pointers. Translate what Izzy is saying so that Larry can understand.

1. I know it can be a **pain in the neck** learning your way around.

_____

2. Don't get **down in the dumps** if you don't figure it out right away.

_____

3. You'll **have your hands full** for a little while.

_____

4. But just **hang on** and it will get easier.

_____

5. You'll be **up and running** before you know it.

_____

6. You can **bet your bottom dollar** you're going to like it here.

_____

7. Keep an eye out for me if you have any questions!

_____

8. I have a feeling we're going to be like **two peas in a pod**.

_____

U.S. Presidents

To complete each sentence below, fill in the name of the correct president from the word bank.

> Thomas Jefferson   Barack Obama   Richard Nixon   Abraham Lincoln
> James Monroe   Theodore Roosevelt   George Washington
> John F. Kennedy   Grover Cleveland   Ronald Reagan

1. _____ issued the Emancipation Proclamation, which freed the slaves.

2. _____ was the only president to resign from office.

3. _____ acted in fifty-three films before becoming involved in politics.

4. _____ was the first president of the United States and is on the dollar bill.

5. _____ was the first African American president.

6. _____ was the youngest president elected. He was assassinated while still in office.

7. _____ doubled the size of our country with the Louisiana Purchase.

8. _____ was the only president to serve two nonconsecutive terms.

9. _____ is best known for the Monroe Doctrine, his contribution to U.S. foreign policy.

10. _____ is known for using the expression "Speak softly and carry a big stick."

Missing Angles

For each shape below, there is one angle that is not given. Use the information you have to determine the missing angle for each shape.

1. Angle A = _____
Angle B = 48°
Angle C = 48°

2. Angle R = 80°
Angle S = 80°
Angle T = _____
Angle U = 100°

3. Angle X = _____
Angle Y = 30°

4. Angle F = 47°
Angle G = 79°
Angle H = 95°
Angle I = _____

5. Angle O = 38°
Angle P = _____
Angle Q = 99°

6. Angle K = 140°
Angle L = 82°
Angle M = _____
Angle N = 85°

7. Angle E = 105°
Angle F = _____
Angle G = 33°

8. Angle T = _____
Angle U = 68°
Angle V = 119°
Angle W = 106°

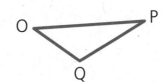

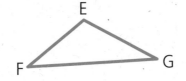

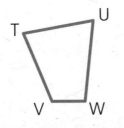

Timely Trains

Use the train schedule to answer the questions.

Trains	A	B	C	D	E
Charlotte	7:15	8:10	9:05	10:38	12:20
Wilson	8:20	9:15	10:10	11:43	1:25
Daisy Falls	9:05	10:30	10:55	12:28	2:10
Redding	9:47	11:12	11:37	1:10	2:52
Ashton	11:28	12:23	1:18	2:51	4:33
Franklin	1:35	3:00	3:25	4:58	6:40
Storyville	2:55	4:20	4:45	6:18	8:00

1. How long does it take to get from Wilson to Ashton? _____

2. How long does it take to get from Daisy Falls to Storyville? _____

3. You took Train B from Wilson to Ashton. Then you picked up Train C to Franklin. How long did you spend on the train? _____

4. You took Train D from Charlotte to Redding. Then you picked up Train E to Storyville. How long was your trip from beginning to end? _____

5. How long is the wait in Ashton between Train A and Train D? _____

Mixed-Up Medleys

Someone has mixed up all the lyrics to familiar patriotic songs.
Circle the words that are wrong and write the correct words above them.

"America the Boastful"

O beautiful for spacious flies,

For ample waves of brains,

For orange mountain tragedies,

Above the freighted trains!

"I'm a Yankee Doodle Handy"

I'm a Yankee Doodle Handy,

A Yankee Doodle, dude am I

A real life cousin of my uncle Ben

Born on the Eighth of July.

"My Country 'Tis of Three"

My country tis of three,

Sweet man of liberty,

Of these we sing.

Land where my fathers flied!

Band of the Pilgrim's ride!

From every mountain sighed,

Let freedom bring!

"This Hand Is Your Hand"

This hand is your hand,

This hand is my hand,

From California

To the Hawaiian Islands,

This hand was paid for you and me.

Weather Crossword

Use the clues about weather to fill in the crossword puzzle with words from the word bank.
Use the internet or a dictionary to find the meaning of each word.

> convection current   wind   hurricane   atmosphere
> global winds   occluded   station model
> cold   stationary   tornado

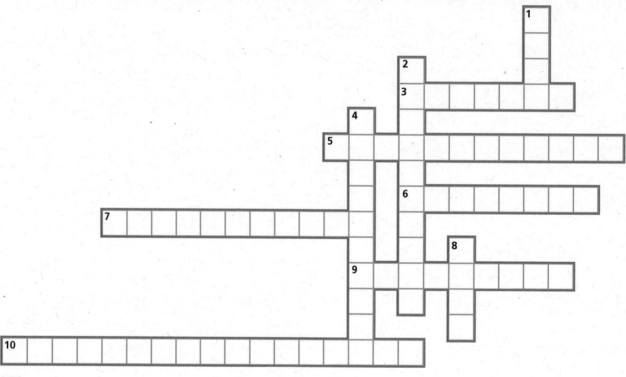

Across

3. a dark funnel of strong winds that spiral upward

5. a standard system of symbols that shows the current weather conditions at a particular weather reporting station (2 words)

6. the type of front that brings light rain and milder temperatures

7. steady winds that blow over long distances from a specific direction (2 words)

9. a very large, violent tropical storm that gains energy from warm, moist, rising air

10. the circular movement of air or water caused by uneven heating (2 words)

Down

1. the type of front that brings clouds and rain

2. the type of front that can produce gusty winds

4. the blanket of air that surrounds Earth

8. the horizontal movement of air

Flurries of Fun

The graph shows how many inches of snow fell each winter for five years.
Use the graph to answer the questions below.

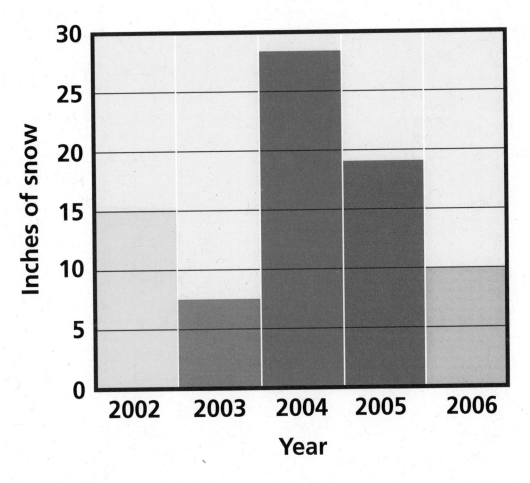

1. What information appears on the *x*-axis? _____

2. What information appears on the *y*-axis? _____

3. Which year had the most snow? _____

4. Which year had the least amount of snow? _____

5. Which month had $\frac{1}{4}$ as many inches of snow as 2004?_____

6. Which month had almost 50% more snow than 2006? _____

Prime Factors

Fill in the missing numbers from the factor trees below.

1.

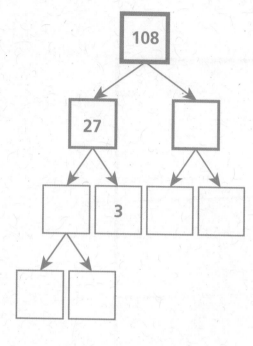

2.

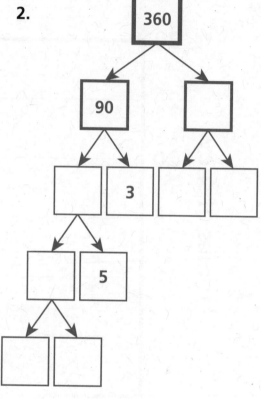

3.

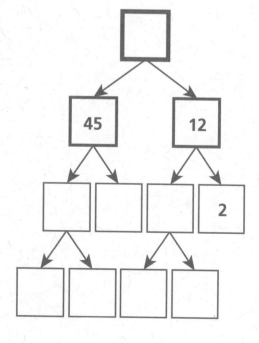

4.

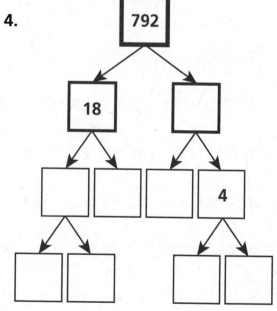

Words Often Confused

The words in the word bank are frequently confused with one another.
Use the words in the word bank to complete the sentences below.

> then   affect   breath   capital   capitol   effect   principal
> principle   stationary   breathe   stationery   than

1. Boston is the _____ of Massachusetts.

2. I flossed my teeth, _____ I brushed them.

3. Sheila bought new _____ to write letters to her cousin.

4. This flavor of ice cream is better _____ this one.

5. I take a _____ and inhale the sweet scent of a rose.

6. Lack of sleep will _____ your ability to concentrate.

7. The middle school has a new assistant _____ this year.

8. Is the sculpture _____ or can it be moved?

9. If you _____ out when it's cold, you'll see a white cloud of vapor in the air.

10. The state _____ needs a new roof.

11. Cavities are an _____ of not taking care of your teeth.

12. On _____ I cannot do that; it goes against my beliefs.

Puzzling Race

The neighborhood kids are having a race to see who can get more of a puzzle done in 20 minutes. Since all of the kids are different ages, the older kids get puzzles with more pieces, while the younger kids get puzzles with fewer pieces. Determine what fraction of the puzzle each child finished. Reduce the fraction to lowest terms and convert it to a percentage. Round decimals to the nearest hundredth. The first one is done for you.

Name	Number of Pieces in Puzzle	Number of Pieces Put Together of Puzzle	Fraction of Puzzle Completed	Percentage of Puzzle Completed
Lily	55	44	$\frac{4}{5}$	$\frac{4}{5} = 0.80$ .080 X 100= 80%
Omar	132	88		
Olivia	212	159		
Hasid	24	8		
Mary	300	270		
Morgan	82	41		
Irene	91	52		
Terrence	260	104		

Who won the race? _____.

Story Setting

Suppose you are writing a story that is set in your bedroom. You need to describe your **setting** well in order to give your reader a clear idea of what it looks like. Answer the questions below.

1. First, make a drawing of your bedroom. Include things like furniture, doors, and windows.

2. Now, use your senses to write a paragraph about your bedroom. What would a person see in your room? What would he or she hear? What does it smell like? Use good detail words.

_____

_____

_____

_____

_____

_____

_____

_____

Share your drawing and description with people who have been in your room and see if they think you've done a good job describing it.

Track a Thunderstorm

The next time there is a thunderstorm approaching your area, you can impress your friends and family by telling them how far away it is.

Here's what you'll need:
- thunderstorm
- stopwatch

Here's what you do:

1. Wait for a flash of lightning.

2. Use the stopwatch (or count, if you can't find a stopwatch) to find the number of seconds until you hear thunder.

Every five seconds is one mile. So, divide the number of seconds by 5 to see how many miles away the storm is. Complete this chart to help you:

Seconds	5	10	15	20	25	30	35	40	45
Miles	1								

Why it works:

Believe it or not, lightning and thunder happen at the same time. Since light travels faster than sound, light (the lightning) is seen instantly, while sound (the thunder) takes longer to reach your ear. The closer together the thunder and lightning are, the closer the storm is to you.

Decimal Fraction Comparisons

Solve the word problems below by converting the fractions to decimals or the decimals to fractions.

1. Kelly's cat weighs 9.4 pounds and her dog weighs $9\frac{1}{3}$ pounds. Which animal weighs more? _____

2. Vincent's cousin lives 11.7 miles away. His brother lives $11\frac{9}{10}$ miles away. Which of Vincent's relatives lives closer? _____

3. A grocery store is having a sale in which a gallon of milk is 15% off. A country store across town is having a sale in which a gallon of milk is $\frac{1}{5}$ off. If a gallon of milk normally costs the same amount at the two stores, then which store is having the better sale? _____

4. Inga's mother is 7.8 inches taller than Inga. Inga's father is $7\frac{3}{5}$ inches taller than Inga. Who is taller, Inga's mother or her father? _____

5. Lee is 3.27 years older than Clive. Omar is $3\frac{1}{4}$ years older than Clive. Who is younger, Lee or Omar? _____

6. Min and Asa both have flower gardens that are 10 feet wide. Min's vegetable garden is 1.5 times wider than her flower garden. Asa's vegetable garden is $1\frac{3}{7}$ times wider than his flower garden. Whose vegetable garden is wider? _____

7. Milo's painting is 10.68 inches tall and his clay sculpture is $10\frac{5}{7}$ inches tall. Which piece of art is taller? _____

8. Nina can lift $\frac{8}{9}$ of her weight. Fiona can lift .84 times her weight. Who can lift more weight? _____

Troublesome Verbs

Read the definitions of verbs that are often confused. Then circle the correct word in each sentence.

Lie means "to rest in a flat position" or "to be in a certain place."
Lay means "to place."

Sit means "to occupy a seat."
Set means "to place."

Rise means "to go upward."
Raise means "to lift or to make something go up."

1. I'm going to (lie/lay) down for a nap.

2. Did the story (rise/raise) any questions for you?

3. Please (lie/lay) the coats on the bed.

4. (Sit/Set) your things down over there.

5. Would you like to (sit/set) for a few minutes?

6. My father (raises/rises) at seven every morning.

7. The sleepy kitten likes to (lie/lay) on the bed.

8. I will (sit/set) a spot for you at dinner.

Quadrants

Graph the following ordered pairs. Then tell which quadrant the point falls in.

1. (4,–7) _____

2. (–2,6) _____

3. (2,3) _____

4. (–5,–3) _____

5. (4,–2) _____

6. (5,3) _____

7. (–3,–1) _____

8. (–8,3) _____

State Smarts

Use the map and the key to answer the questions.

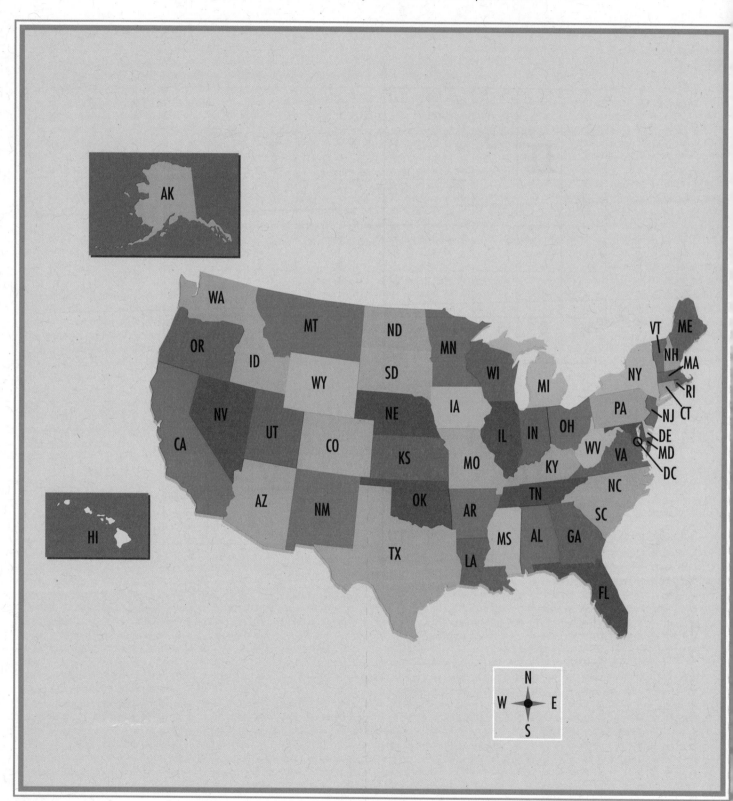

1. Which state lies east of Arizona? _____

2. Which state lies north of Oregon? _____

3. Which state lies south of South Dakota?_____

4. Which state lies west of Alabama? _____

5. Which state lies north of Iowa?_____

6. Which state lies west of Nevada? _____

7. Which state lies north of New Mexico? _____

8. Which state lies east of Tennessee? _____

9. Which state lies south of Kansas? _____

10. Which state lies north of Wyoming? _____

11. Which state lies south of Georgia? _____

12. Which state lies north of Connecticut? _____

13. Which two states lie west of Idaho? _____

14. Which two states lie north of Florida?_____

15. Which two states lie south of Massachusetts?_____

16. Which state lies on the northeast tip of the United States? _____

Similes and Metaphors

A **simile** compares two things using the words *like* or *as*. A **metaphor** compares two things without using *like* or *as*. Look at the example in the box. Then write whether each sentence below contains a simile or a metaphor.

Simile	The clouds look just like cotton candy.
Metaphor	The clouds are cotton candy puffs.

1. This pear is as sweet as honey. _____

2. My cat is as fast as the wind. _____

3. The bar of soap is a slippery fish. _____

4. My brother is as big as a bear. _____

5. The sun is a giant fireball. _____

6. My new teacher is a breath of fresh air. _____

7. Harold's little sister is a princess. _____

8. This candy is as hard as a rock. _____

Finish these sentences below to create your own similes.

9. My smile is as wide as _____.

10. The dog's fur is soft like _____.

Finish these sentences below to create your own metaphors.

11. The choppy ocean is _____.

12. After a long day, my pillow is _____.

Happy Hyberbole

Hyperbole is an obvious exaggeration used by an author. A hyperbole is not literally true but is used to emphasize something. Look at the example in the box.
Then underline the hyperbole in each sentence below.

> My father's feet are **as big as a house.**

1. I walk a million miles to get to school each day.

2. We waited forever for our movie to begin.

3. Sarah's so smart, her brain is as big as an elephant.

4. It took me a million years to make breakfast this morning.

5. Marc ran as fast as light in the race.

6. I was so upset, I cried for weeks.

7. If I don't get a new coat before school starts, I will die!

8. The library has a billion books for me to borrow.

Now finish each sentence to create your own hyperboles.

9. These books weigh _____.

10. I'm so hungry I could _____.

11. Harry waited _____ to board his plane.

12. Abigail is so tall, she _____.

Punctuation Pirate

All of the internal punctuation marks are missing from the story below. Add in the colons, commas, and quotation marks to complete the story. Then answer the questions that follow.

This morning I did not wake up until 730. My alarm went off at 710 but I was up late last night reading a short story called Tales of the High Seas. My favorite line in the story was when the captain says Walk the plank! to the prisoner. Then the pirates sang Life on the Seas. There are three things I like about the story the way the pirates talk the adventures they go on and the interesting places they go. When I get home from school I have to do my homework do my chores and eat dinner. Then I will read the story Mutiny at Midnight. The pirates in that story are Bluebeard Pegleg Pete and One-Eyed Wally.

1. What two ways are colons used in this story? _____

_____

2. What two ways are quotation marks used?_____

_____

3. What two ways are commas used? _____

_____

Make It Rain

Impress friends and family by making it rain! Follow the instructions below to complete the activity.

Here's what you'll need:
- large glass jar with a wide mouth, like a mayonnaise jar
- hot water
- ice cubes
- small plate to put ice cubes on

Here's what you do:

1. Pour two inches of very hot tap water in the jar.

2. Put the plate on top of the jar.

3. Wait a few minutes.

4. Place the ice cubes on the plate.

What happens? _____

_____

Why it works:
The cold plate makes the moisture in the warm air in the jar condense to form water droplets.

How does this compare with what you know about air in the atmosphere? _____

_____

_____

Allowances

Calvin and his friends each receive a different amount of weekly allowance.
How long would it take each person to save up for the item listed? Complete the chart below.
The first one is done for you.

Allowance Per Week	A Book Costing $7.50	A CD Costing $9.95	A New Game Costing $14.75	A Pack of New Pencils Costing $2.88	A New Toy Costing $4.99	A New Movie Costing $18.45	A Telescope Costing $27.30	A Calculator Costing $12.20
$1.50	5 weeks							
$1.85								
$2.25								
$3.30								
$3.65								
$4.85								

Rooting Around

Use the roots in the box to find words that match the meanings given below.

> *auto* means "self"
>
> *trans* means "across"
>
> *port* means "to carry" or "to bear"
>
> *graph* means "to write"
>
> *tele* means "distance, from afar"

1. Write a word that means "a person's own signature." _____

2. Write a word that means "to carry from one place to another." _____

3. Write a word that means "a system for transmitting messages to a distant place."

_____

4. Write a word that means "to move a body by telekinesis."_____

5. Write a word that means "to bring in from a foreign country." _____

6. Write a word that means "able to start, operate, move, etc., on its own."_____

7. Write a word that means "the story of one's own life." _____

8. See how many English words you can think of that use the roots above.

_____

_____

_____

_____

_____

_____

_____

_____

Circular Products

Write the product of the numbers in the circles where they overlap. The first one has been done for you. Round all answers to the nearest thousandth.

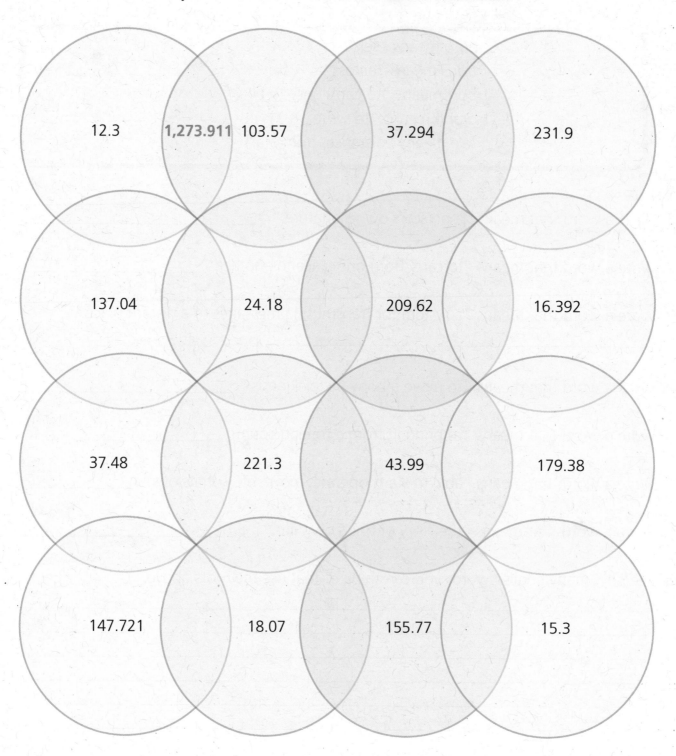

12.3   **1,273.911**   103.57   37.294   231.9

137.04   24.18   209.62   16.392

37.48   221.3   43.99   179.38

147.721   18.07   155.77   15.3

Letter by Letter

Change the words below to their opposites by changing one letter at a time.

Example:
F O R E
B O R E
B A R E
B A R K
B A C K

1.
MARE

___ ___ ___ ___

___ ___ ___ ___

___ ___ ___ ___

___ ___ ___ ___

COLT

2.
RISE

___ ___ ___ ___

___ ___ ___ ___

___ ___ ___ ___

FALL

3.
DULL

___ ___ ___ ___

___ ___ ___ ___

KEEN

4.
WILD

___ ___ ___ ___

___ ___ ___ ___

TAME

Now draw a line to match the words to their opposites.

tall	fat
skinny	dirty
bad	short
old	sour
sweet	good
clean	young

Almost Equal

There is something wrong with the number rectangles below. The sum of the top three rows is supposed to add up to the sum of the bottom row. Find and cross out a number in one of the top three rows to make the sums equal.

1.

0.51	3.4	1.1	2.09
0.99	2.73	1.94	3.0
1.7	1.33	2.3	0.79
4.8	5.12	6.93	3.7

2.

1.03	0.93	2.48	3.2
0.09	2.18	2.61	1.85
0.77	1.5	1.24	3.08
6.01	3.27	4.0	5.5

3.

1.39	2.41	0.84	1.03
4.6	6.1	2.67	3.17
5.2	2.88	0.48	1.94
8.42	5.19	7.4	10.31

4.

3.69	2.72	5.3	4.31
3.93	5.8	3.94	5.37
2.91	1.45	3.04	2.3
11.49	8.73	14.01	6.22

5.

11.05	4.3	12.44	9.7
5.21	2.23	6.47	3.18
7.52	4.45	5.85	3.9
27.3	12.83	23.2	5.45

6.

6.4	8.21	7.1	10.3
12.37	9.5	3.94	5.74
10.0	8.61	5.9	10.4
31.29	24.8	15.22	20.06

School Supplies

Use the prices of the school supplies in the box to answer the questions below.

pencils $1.85	notebook $2.55
pencil sharpener $1.25	folders $1.80
crayons $3.35	pens $2.05

1. Callan has $9.80. Which four items can he buy and have no money left over?

_____   _____   _____   _____

2. Sheree has $6.95. Which four items can she buy?

_____   _____   _____   _____

3. David has $8.95. Which four items can he buy and have no money left over?

_____   _____   _____   _____

4. Jordie has $8.45. Which four items can she buy and have no money left over?

_____   _____   _____   _____

5. Ralph has $5.00. If he buys pencils and folders, how much money does he have left over?

_____

6. Celia has $7.50. If she buys crayons and a notebook, how much money does she have left over?_____

7. Felicia has $6.80. If she buys pens and pencils, how much money does she have left?

_____

8. Jose has $8.27. If he buys pencils, a notebook, and pens, how much money does he have left? _____

9. Marcie has 50% of the amount needed to buy folders. How much money does she have?

_____

10. Sammy has 20% of the amount needed to buy a pencil sharpener. How much money does he have? _____

37

Plant Pipes

Try this experiment to see how the xylem and phloem pipelines in a plant work.

Here's what you'll need:
- leafy stalk of celery
- knife
- cup of water
- colored food dye

Here's what you do:

1. Cut a thin slice from the bottom of the celery and throw that slice away.

2. Add the food coloring to the water.

3. Place the cut end of the celery in the cup of water.

4. Let it sit for half an hour or so.

5. Break the celery apart lengthwise.

What part of the stalk is colored? _____

Can you follow the path the coloring took through the stalk? _____

Did any coloring reach the leaves? _____

_____

_____

Why do you think the color traveled through the plant? _____

_____

_____

Pretty Palindromes

A **palindrome** is a word or phrase that reads the same backward and forward. Look at the examples in the box. Then write a palindrome that completes each sentence.

race car	kayak	level
radar	stats	madam

1. My cheeks are red, but yours are _____ _____ _____ _____ _____ _____.

2. When babies eat, they wear a _____ _____ _____.

3. Another word for *looks* is _____ _____ _____ _____.

4. The sun is directly overhead at _____ _____ _____ _____.

5. You should try to do a good _____ _____ _____ _____ every day.

6. Be quiet; don't make a _____ _____ _____ _____.

7. Some people believe in an eye for an _____ _____ _____.

8. See what other palindromes you can come up with.

_____

_____

_____

_____

_____

_____

Homophones Crossword

Homophones are words that are pronounced the same but have different meanings and spellings. Use homophones to fill in the crossword below.

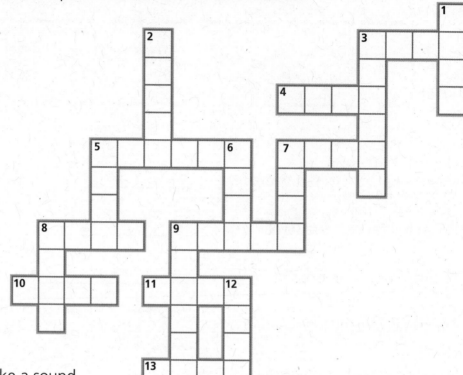

Across

3. a place next to

4. to cause a bell to make a sound

5. greater height

7. a part in a play or situation

8. to run away

9. crushes or grinds with the teeth

10. to appear to be, feel, do, etc.

11. small piece of bread

13. an unintended hole or crack that lets water in

Down

1. place where two pieces of cloth are sewn together

2. to get all the water out by twisting

3. to have let out one's breath with a sound

5. to give someone a job

6. stood up

7. lines of people or things

8. a small insect, often on a dog

9. to select freely

12. vegetable like a large green onion

Write a Haiku

A **haiku** is a type of Japanese poem. It has three lines. The first and last lines have five syllables, and the middle line has seven syllables. It does not rhyme. Haiku usually have a seasonal reference. See the example of a haiku in the box.

> Green leaves on the tree,
> Blowing in the mighty wind,
> Summer is ending.

Now think of a subject on which to write your own haiku. Remember to use five syllables in the first and last lines and seven syllables in the middle line. Draw a picture in the box below to illustrate your haiku.

_____

_____

_____

Double Check

Terry has finished her test early. She wants to double check her answers before she turns in the test. Can you help Terry check her test and fix any mistakes she may have made?

1. −19 + −34 = −53

2. 54 + 72 = 116

3. −42 − 20 = −22

4. 27 + −13 = 14

5. −56 + −23 = −33

6. −38 −19 = −57

7. 78 + 45 = 123

8. −29 + −18 = −11

9. −59 −31 = 90

10. 53 + −66 = 119

11. 32 + − 46 = −14

12. −41 − −15 = 26

Do Leaves Give Off Water?

Try this experiment to find out if leaves give off water.

Here's what you'll need:
- clear plastic bags
- tape

Here's what you do:
1. Carefully place a bag over the end of a tree branch.
2. Tape it closed around the branch.
3. Place bags on other trees and plants in the same way.
4. Look at the bags after a few hours and again the next day.

What you observed:

1. What happened in the bags? _____

2. Where does the moisture come from? _____

3. Did all of the plants give off the same amount of water?_____

4. Do you think the kind of day (sunny, cloudy, humid, foggy) affects how much water comes off the leaves? _____

5. How do you know that the moisture came from the leaves?_____
_____

6. Why do plant leaves give off water?_____

Family Reunion

The Leonard family is having a family reunion. Each relative flew on a plane for part of the trip and drove a car for the other part of the trip. Can you figure out how many miles each relative traveled to get to the reunion? Round decimals to the nearest tenth. The first one is done for you.

Relative	Distance Traveled	Total Miles
Uncle Bob	270 miles in a plane + $\frac{2}{3}$ as many miles in a car	270 × $\frac{2}{3}$ = 180 miles (by car) 270 miles (by plane) 270 + 180 = 450 miles (total)
Grandma Elaine	397 miles in a car + $\frac{1}{2}$ as many miles in a plane	
Cousin Justine	180 miles in a car + $\frac{5}{6}$ as many miles in a plane	
Great-aunt Ann	549 miles in a plane + $\frac{2}{7}$ as many miles in a car	
Aunt Joan	403 miles in a car + $\frac{2}{5}$ as many miles in a plane	
Cousin Larry	730 miles in a plane + $\frac{1}{10}$ as many miles in a car	
Grandpa Louis	652 miles in a car + $\frac{3}{8}$ as many in a plane	
Cousin Skylar	475 miles in a plane + $\frac{2}{9}$ as many in a car	

Who traveled the farthest to get to the reunion? _____

Body-Part Anagrams

Anagrams are words made by using the letters of a word in a different order. Look at the examples in the box. Then figure out which body part each of the words below is an anagram for.

are = ear	race = care	alert = later
ache = each	act = cat	large = regal

1. earth _____

2. impart _____

3. waits _____

4. fringe _____

5. below_____

6. limped _____

7. lamp _____

8. inch _____

Now see what other anagrams you can come up with.

9. _____

10. _____

11. _____

12. _____

Fraction Riddle

To find out the answer to the riddle, complete the multiplication and division problems below. Write the answers on the lines, then match each answer to its corresponding letter. Show answers in lowest terms.

$R = \dfrac{1}{5} \times \dfrac{1}{3} = $ _____

$H = \dfrac{2}{7} \div \dfrac{1}{3} = $ _____

$N = \dfrac{3}{4} \times \dfrac{4}{9} = $ _____

$I = \dfrac{1}{2} \div \dfrac{3}{5} = $ _____

$Y = \dfrac{5}{6} \times \dfrac{2}{10} = $ _____

$T = \dfrac{3}{44} \div \dfrac{3}{11} = $ _____

$E = \dfrac{5}{13} \times \dfrac{2}{3} = $ _____

How far is it from the sun to the earth?

The Earth is _____ _____ _____ _____ _____ _____ - _____ _____ _____ _____ _____

$\dfrac{1}{3}$ $\quad$ $\dfrac{5}{6}$ $\quad$ $\dfrac{1}{3}$ $\quad$ $\dfrac{10}{39}$ $\quad$ $\dfrac{1}{4}$ $\quad$ $\dfrac{1}{6}$ $\quad$ $\dfrac{1}{4}$ $\quad$ $\dfrac{6}{7}$ $\quad$ $\dfrac{1}{15}$ $\quad$ $\dfrac{10}{39}$ $\quad$ $\dfrac{10}{39}$

million miles away from the sun!

Terrific Titles

A title should be both informative and interesting. If you were to write a nonfiction report, the title would be different from a title for a fictional story. Write a title that will capture a reader's attention for each topic below.

1. a report on ponds _____

2. a story about three friends at summer camp _____

3. a report on making paper _____

4. an explanation of how a microwave works _____

5. a science fiction story about traveling to a new planet _____

6. a mystery about a missing painting _____

7. an explanation of how money is made _____

8. a report on your family's customs _____

9. a story about a young girl's first day of school _____

10. a biography of Abraham Lincoln's life _____

Digestive System

Each of the scrambled words below is a part of the digestive system. Unscramble the words, then use them to label the diagram of the digestive system.

1. asapecrn _____

2. spaeuhgso _____

3. ntterieelignsa _____

4. eturmc _____

5. toumh _____

6. siagnalrdyslva _____

7. smchtoa _____

8. erliv _____

9. smltenletisani _____

10. dblaeraldlg _____

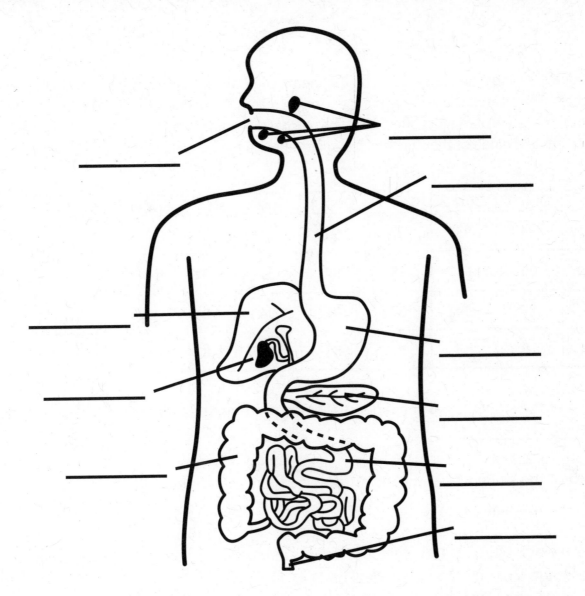

Now write each part in the order that food travels through the digestive system.

11. _____

12. _____

13. _____

14. _____

15. _____

16. _____

Help the Teacher

Mr. McDonald is almost finished calculating the **mean**, **median**, and **mode** of each of his students' quiz scores. The mean is the average number. The median is the middle number. The mode is the number that is repeated most often. Help the teacher by completing the chart with the mean, median, and mode of the students' test scores. Round the answers to the nearest tenth.

Name	Quiz 1	Quiz 2	Quiz 3	Quiz 4	Quiz 5	Quiz 6	Mean	Median	Mode
Geoffrey	84	93	89	93	81	85			
Celeste	95	91	85	87	86	91			
Jose	87	94	87	91	94	94			
Raven	79	85	90	85	93	82			

1. Which of the students has the highest average score on the quizzes?

_____

2. Which of the students has the lowest average score on the quizzes?

_____

3. If the average score for the other 16 students in the class was 92 for Quiz 1, what was the average score for the whole class on Quiz 1?

_____

4. What is the median score for all the grades shown in the chart?

_____

Tackling Topics

When you choose a topic to write about, you have to make sure it is not too broad or too general. Choose one of the topics in the box. Then narrow the topic by answering the questions below.

vehicles   holidays   musical instruments

jobs   clothes   books   animals

1. Who? _____

2. What? _____

3. When? _____

4. Where? _____

5. Why? _____

6. How? _____

Specific topic: _____

Now write a paragraph about the topic you have chosen.

_____
_____
_____
_____
_____
_____
_____
_____
_____

Name the State

Use each of the clues below to determine which U.S. state is being described.

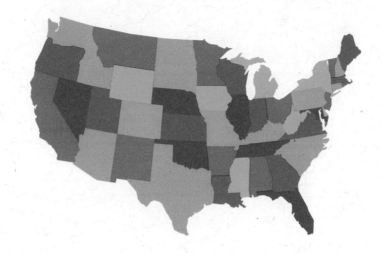

1. This state has a **tan** in it. _____

2. This state has an **ark** in it. _____

3. This state has a **lab** in it. _____

4. This state has a **color** in it. _____

5. This state has a **ham** in it. _____

6. This state has a **cut** in it. _____

7. This state has a **law** in it. _____

8. This state has a **van** in it. _____

9. This state has a backward **axe** in it. _____

10. This state has a backward **hat** in it. _____

11. This state has a backward **nag** in it. _____

12. This state has a backward **had** in it. _____

Improper Fractions

Kathy was looking over her test answers and noticed that the directions asked for all answers to be written as mixed numbers in lowest terms. Unfortunately Kathy has written all her answers as improper fractions. Help Kathy convert all of her answers to mixed numbers. Show all fractions in lowest terms.

1. $\dfrac{14}{5}$ = _____

2. $\dfrac{8}{2}$ = _____

3. $\dfrac{11}{3}$ = _____

4. $\dfrac{21}{6}$ = _____

5. $\dfrac{37}{8}$ = _____

6. $\dfrac{44}{7}$ = _____

7. $\dfrac{17}{2}$ = _____

8. $\dfrac{29}{5}$ = _____

9. $\dfrac{84}{9}$ = _____

10. $\dfrac{147}{10}$ = _____

11. $\dfrac{87}{13}$ = _____

12. $\dfrac{60}{15}$ = _____

Out of Order

Number the steps below to put them in the correct order.

_____ Put the card into an envelope.

_____ Fold a blank sheet of colored paper in half.

_____ Color in your design and write the greeting.

_____ Fold the paper in half again to make quarters.

_____ Choose or make an envelope for the card.

_____ Draw a design on the folded card.

Now use the steps to write a paragraph about a card you would like to create. Explain in detail how you would decorate it. Don't forget transition words and a catchy title!

_____

_____

_____

_____

_____

_____

Severe Search

There are 16 words related to severe weather in the word search below. Find and circle the words. Then write them on the lines as you find them.

G	W	O	N	S	H	X	O	P	V	D	B	S	S	I
G	N	F	U	Y	R	U	D	O	Q	L	M	M	G	V
N	H	I	V	P	X	P	S	B	M	C	I	P	L	F
G	O	E	N	A	C	I	R	R	U	H	D	A	G	X
T	L	X	Q	T	X	L	K	N	M	J	P	W	H	S
N	L	I	H	U	H	N	O	O	S	N	O	M	A	U
O	A	B	I	O	T	G	U	D	Q	B	D	N	N	G
R	U	L	R	P	B	E	I	T	V	P	D	Q	I	D
R	Q	I	E	S	S	M	E	L	X	S	L	O	E	R
E	S	Z	T	R	K	I	I	L	T	B	D	I	N	Z
D	J	Z	S	E	H	E	V	O	S	A	E	C	O	L
N	S	A	I	T	Y	P	R	I	N	C	L	E	L	D
U	X	R	W	A	I	M	E	R	O	N	O	S	C	N
H	A	D	T	W	A	J	O	U	W	S	C	Z	Y	I
T	H	G	R	Q	T	T	M	X	N	E	E	Q	C	W

_____ _____ _____ _____

_____ _____ _____ _____

_____ _____ _____ _____

_____ _____ _____ _____

Kelsey's Quickest Path

Kelsey is late! She missed the bus to school and needs to find the quickest way to get there. Follow the path of prime numbers to get her to school as fast as possible.

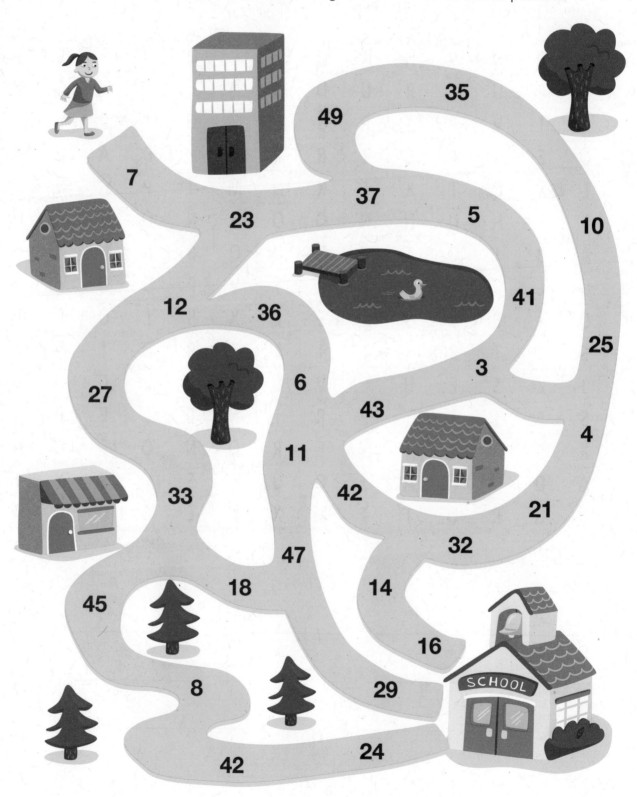

Sensory Search

Sensory language makes writing more vivid. An author chooses words carefully to make the reader see, hear, touch, taste, and smell what is happening in a story. The words in the word bank are sensory words. Write each word in the column below where it belongs.

ripe	glowing	warm	boom	snap
fuzzy	bitter	fishy	wrinkled	damp
buzz	smooth	bumpy	salty	musty
curved	immense	whisper	tangy	fragrant

Sight	Hearing	Touch	Taste	Smell

Now write your own sensory words.

Sight	Hearing	Touch	Taste	Smell

What's for Dinner?

Use the information given to rewrite the recipe.

Salsa Chicken
serves 4

1 small onion	½ green bell pepper
2 tablespoons olive oil	1 pound chicken legs
2 cups salsa	1 pound spinach
3 cups cooked brown rice	½ tsp salt
¼ tsp pepper	1 Tbsp red pepper flakes

1. Rewrite this recipe to serve 8 people.

2. Rewrite this recipe to serve 6 people.

Measuring Mandy

Mandy needs to find out a few measurements around the house for a school project. Help Mandy take the measurements by writing in what the most appropriate units of measurement would be to measure each given object. Use the list of units of measurement in the word bank below.

Units of Measurement

gallons   square feet   inches   square inches
feet   cubic feet   miles   cubic inches   cups   acres

---

1. The perimeter of Mandy's house: _____

2. The capacity of Mandy's bathtub: _____

3. The volume of Mandy's fridge: _____

4. The amount of land Mandy's house is on: _____

5. The area of Mandy's living room: _____

6. The amount of liquid that Mandy's hat could hold: _____

7. The area of a piece of paper: _____

8. The volume of a shoebox: _____

9. The distance between Mandy's house and school: _____

10. The length of a fork: _____

Magnet Mystery

Use a magnet to test different objects for attraction.

Here's what you'll need:
- magnet
- objects to test (see chart below)

Here's what you do:
1. Make a prediction about each object.
2. Place each object next to the magnet to see if it will be attracted.
3. Record your observations.

Why it works:
A magnet attracts metals, such as iron and steel.

Object	Prediction	Magnetic/Nonmagnetic
Nickel		
Paper		
Penny		
Metal Spoon		
Plastic Fork		
Paper Clip		
Popsicle Stick		
Toothbrush		
Paper Plate		
Nail		
Mirror		
Masking Tape		

Now sort the objects you tested into the correct category.

Magnetic Items	Nonmagnetic Items

What do the magnetic items have in common?_____

What do the nonmagnetic items have in common? _____

_____

What are some other objects that you think would be magnetic? _____

_____

What are some other objects that you know are nonmagnetic? _____

_____

Prize Pumpkins

A class grew pumpkins and kept track of their weight over eight weeks. The teacher didn't specify which unit of measurement to use so all of the measurements are different. Fill in the empty chart with the conversions of the weights to pounds. Then answer the questions that follow.

Name	Week 1	Week 2	Week 3	Week 4	Week 5	Week 6	Week 7	Week 8
Liu	2.5 lbs	5 lbs	8.75 lbs	11 lbs	14 lbs	17.5 lbs	21.25 lbs	24.4 lbs
Gregor	20 oz	36 oz	68 oz	98.3 oz	131.5 oz	164.9 oz	193.4 oz	211.5 oz
Janice	1.2 kg	2.3 kg	4.1 kg	4.9 kg	6.3 kg	7.5 kg	8.8 kg	10.1 kg
Juan	2 lbs 4 oz	4 lbs 3 oz	7 lbs 2 oz	10 lbs 7 oz	12 lbs 5 oz	16 lbs 8 oz	19 lbs 1 oz	22 lbs 7 oz
Ivan	1,100 g	1,950 g	4,375 g	4,855 g	5,730 g	7,390 g	8,650 g	9,595 g

Name	Week 1	Week 2	Week 3	Week 4	Week 5	Week 6	Week 7	Week 8
Liu	2.5 lbs	5 lbs	8.75 lbs	11 lbs	14 lbs	17.5 lbs	21.25 lbs	24.4 lbs
Gregor								
Janice								
Juan								
Ivan								

1. Which student's pumpkin grew the most between week 4 and week 5?

_____

2. Which student's pumpkin was the heaviest in week 2?

_____

3. Which student's pumpkin was exactly double the weight of another student's pumpkin in week 1? _____

4. Which student's pumpkin was the heaviest in the last week? _____

5. Which two students' pumpkins had a combined weight of more than 18.5 lbs in week 3? _____

6. Which student's pumpkin was the lightest in week 6? _____

7. Which student had the lightest pumpkin every week? _____

8. Which two students' pumpkins weighed 3.5 pounds in week 1? _____

Exciting Endings

Read the beginning of the story below. Then write your own ending to this story, making sure to create a conclusion that fits the beginning that is already written.

The Case of the Missing Scarf

Janelle was late for school, and it was cold. She could not find her scarf anywhere. "Just take mine," her mother said.

Janelle put on her mother's scarf, kissed her cat, Snowball, good-bye, and ran out to catch the bus.

After school, Janelle decided to figure out the mystery of where her scarf went.

_____

_____

_____

_____

_____

_____

_____

_____

The End

Brilliant Beginnings

Read the end of the story below. Then write your own beginning to this story, making sure to create a plot that fits the ending that is already written.

_____

_____

_____

_____

_____

_____

_____

_____

_____

The Treasure Map

To my surprise, there were no jewels or gold coins in the chest. Instead, the map had led me to a chest full of—books! There were all different kinds: mysteries, fantasies, biographies, adventures. It was a treasure I would be enjoying for a long, long time.

The End

Store Sales

Betty's Variety Store and Peter's General Store both sell the same items but in different packages. The charts below show an average week's sales for certain items for each of the stores. Fill in the rest of the charts and answer the questions that follow.

Betty's Variety Store				
Item	Price Per Pack	Price Per Single Item	Packs Sold	Money Made from Packs
4-pack of soup	$3.80	$0.95	11	$41.80
10-pack of juice	$4.99		14	
12-pack of carrots	$2.25		17	
3-pack of bread	$4.00		8	
8-pack of hamburgers	$4.75		13	
4-pack of macaroni	$3.19		5	

66

Peter's General Store				
Item	Price Per Pack	Price Per Single Item	Packs Sold	Money Made from Packs
6-pack of soup	$5.40		7	
8-pack of juice	$3.30		15	
16-pack of carrots	$3.00		12	
4-pack of bread	$4.00		10	
6-pack of hamburgers	$3.79		16	
6-pack of macaroni	$4.39		7	

1. Who made more money from the sale of hamburgers? _____

2. Who made more money from the sale of each single soup? _____

3. Who made more money from the sale of carrots and bread combined? _____

4. How much more money did Peter make from the sale of macaroni than Betty? _____

5. Who sells more juice packs per week? _____

6. Who made the most money this week? _____

Conductors and Insulators

Make an electrical conductivity tester to test objects and see if they are conductors or insulators. Use the chart to first make a prediction about which category an object is in. Then test your prediction and record the results.

Here's what you'll need:
- 1.5-volt battery
- 1.5-volt flashlight bulb
- about 12 inches of bell wire
- knife
- electrical tape
- an adult to help you

Here's what you do:
Make an electrical conductivity tester.
1. With an adult's help, use a knife to cut about an inch of insulation from each end of the wire. Be careful not to cut through the wire.
2. Take the cut insulation off each end of the wire.
3. Twist one of the bare ends of the wire around the base of the flashlight bulb.
4. Tape the other bare end of the wire to the negative (−) side of the battery.
5. Touch the base of the bulb to the positive (+) side of the battery.
6. If you have done it correctly, the bulb should light!
7. Test objects to see if they conduct electricity.
8. Hold a penny between the bulb and the (+) side of the battery.
9. Does the bulb still light?
10. How bright is the light?
11. Record your observations on the chart on the next page.
12. Repeat for other objects.

Why it works:
An electric current, or flow of charged particles, passes from the battery through the wire to light the lightbulb. A conductor allows the electric current to pass through it. An insulator blocks the electric current.

Conductor or Insulator?			
Object	Prediction	No Light, Dim Light, Bright Light, or Very Bright Light?	Conductor or Insulator?
penny			
dime			
pencil			
paper clip			
rubber band			
nail			
leaf			
finger			
piece of plastic			
piece of leather			

Which objects that you tested are the best conductors? _____

_____

Which objects that you tested are the best insulators? _____

_____

Dividing Whole Numbers by Fractions

Solve each word problem below by dividing the fraction into the whole number.

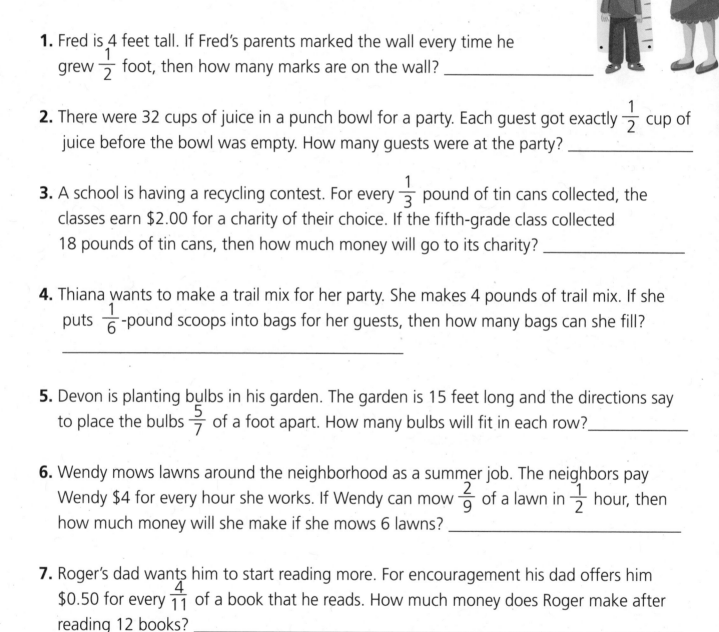

1. Fred is 4 feet tall. If Fred's parents marked the wall every time he grew $\frac{1}{2}$ foot, then how many marks are on the wall? _____

2. There were 32 cups of juice in a punch bowl for a party. Each guest got exactly $\frac{1}{2}$ cup of juice before the bowl was empty. How many guests were at the party? _____

3. A school is having a recycling contest. For every $\frac{1}{3}$ pound of tin cans collected, the classes earn $2.00 for a charity of their choice. If the fifth-grade class collected 18 pounds of tin cans, then how much money will go to its charity? _____

4. Thiana wants to make a trail mix for her party. She makes 4 pounds of trail mix. If she puts $\frac{1}{6}$-pound scoops into bags for her guests, then how many bags can she fill?

_____

5. Devon is planting bulbs in his garden. The garden is 15 feet long and the directions say to place the bulbs $\frac{5}{7}$ of a foot apart. How many bulbs will fit in each row?_____

6. Wendy mows lawns around the neighborhood as a summer job. The neighbors pay Wendy $4 for every hour she works. If Wendy can mow $\frac{2}{9}$ of a lawn in $\frac{1}{2}$ hour, then how much money will she make if she mows 6 lawns? _____

7. Roger's dad wants him to start reading more. For encouragement his dad offers him $0.50 for every $\frac{4}{11}$ of a book that he reads. How much money does Roger make after reading 12 books? _____

8. A baker receives an order for 9 large cakes. It takes the baker 1 tube of frosting to frost $\frac{3}{5}$ of a cake. How many tubes will it take to frost all of the cakes? _____

Silly Story Fill-In

Before you read the story, fill in each blank with any word from the correct part of speech.
Read the silly story you created, then write your own ending.

The year was _____. Chi and his _____ Bob wanted to do something _____.
      year   **noun**   **adjective**

Chi thought of some ideas.

    "We could go to the _____, or we could _____ in the yard, or we could watch a
                 noun   **verb**

_____ movie," he said.
adjective

    They decided they would _____, but first they had to get dressed.
                     verb

    Chi put on a red _____ and _____ shoes. Bob wore a _____. Once they were
                  noun   **adjective**   **noun**

all ready to go, Chi and Bob grabbed a _____.
                          noun

    But before they could leave, Chi's mom asked him if he knew where her _____
                                                noun

was. Chi thought _____. "I think I saw it in the _____," he told her.
             adverb   **noun**

"Maybe _____ knows!"
    name of person

"Thanks, Chi," Mom said. "Make sure you are home in time for _____.
                                    noun

Be here by _____."
    time of the day

    So Chi and Bob went to _____. On the way they saw _____, who was
                    place   **name of person**

holding a bird. When they got there, they couldn't believe their _____. Right
                                      part of body, plural

there in front of them was _____

_____

_____!

Fiction and Nonfiction

Fiction is a type of writing in which a story is created. **Nonfiction**, on the other hand, is based on facts. For each book title below, write whether the book is fiction or nonfiction.

1. *Bobby's Wild UFO Ride* _____

2. *The Day We Adopted a Llama* _____

3. *The War of 1812* _____

4. *My Very Best Friend* _____

5. *A Day in the Life of a Veterinarian* _____

6. *The History of the* Titanic _____

7. *When Frances Met Alex* _____

8. *How to Survive in the Desert* _____

9. *How Many Monkeys in the Tree?* _____

10. *Mummies of Ancient Egypt* _____

11. *The Biography of Lyndon B. Johnson* _____

12. *Carl the Kangaroo* _____

Evaluate Expressions

Write simple one-variable expressions to solve the problems below.

1. If Jake spent 8 hours of the day sleeping, then how many hours of the day was he awake?

_____

2. Chrissie lived in Florida for 100 days out of the year. How many days did she live somewhere else? _____

3. Geoff has 40 comic books. One fourth of the comic books are about superheroes. How many superhero comic books does Geoff have? _____

4. Jill has 2 dogs. There are 3 times the amount of pets in her house than there are dogs. How many pets are in Jill's house? _____

5. Cindy is 3 times the age of her brother, plus 4. If her brother is 5, then how old is Cindy?

_____

6. Kevin made 3 times the amount of money that his brother did, minus 7 dollars. If Kevin made $38, than how much did Kevin's brother make?

_____

7. Nina's father weighs 6 times the sum of Nina's weight and 7. If he weighs 192 pounds, then how much does Nina weigh? _____

8. Drew's baseball-card collection is 5 times the size of Jack's collection, minus 13. If Jack has 27 cards in his collection, then how many cards does Drew have? _____

73

Advertisements

Advertisements are a type of **persuasive writing**. They try to convince you to buy or do things. To create your own advertisement, think about your favorite book. Write three reasons you think someone should read this book (without giving away too much about the book):

1. _____

_____

2. _____

_____

3. _____

_____

Now use what you wrote to draw a poster advertising the book.

Hydrologic Cycle

The **hydrologic cycle**, also known as the water cycle, is the process by which water moves between the oceans, the atmosphere, and the land. Read the definitions below, then use them to label the diagram.

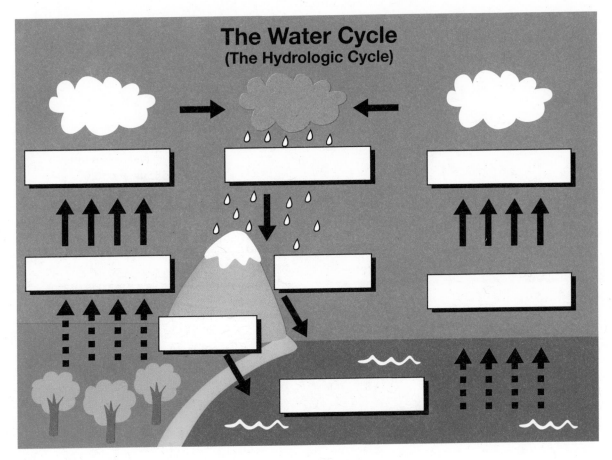

Accumulation is the process in which water gathers in large bodies, such as oceans, seas, and lakes.

Condensation is the process in which water vapor in the air turns into liquid water. Clouds are formed by condensing water. (You will mark this term twice in the diagram.)

Evaporation is the process in which liquid water becomes water vapor. Water vaporizes from the surfaces of lands, bodies of water, and from melting snow.

Precipitation is the process in which water falls from clouds in the sky. Rain and snow are forms of precipitation.

Subsurface runoff is water that drains into underground streams, drains, or sewers.

Surface runoff is water that drains into surface streams, rivers, or canals.

Transpiration is the process in which water from plants evaporates into the atmosphere.

Decimal Pyramids

The pyramids below have some empty boxes. Determine the number pattern for each pyramid and fill in the empty boxes. Start from the top and read left to right to figure out the patterns.

1.

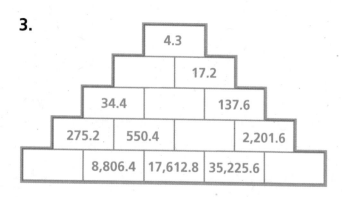

2.

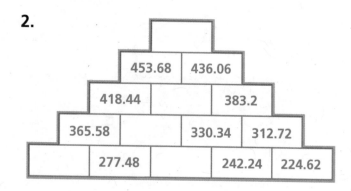

3.

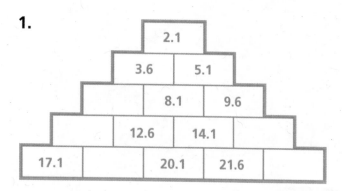

4.

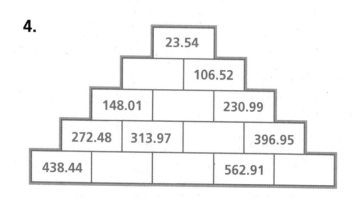

Perfect Patterns

Find the pattern in each sequence of numbers below.

1. 23, 26, 31, 34, 39, 42
Which rule describes this pattern best?

_____

2. 45, 47, 41, 43, 37, 39
Which rule describes this pattern best?

_____

3. 78, 70, 74, 66, 70, 62
Which rule describes this pattern best?

_____

4. 98, 95, 102, 99, 106, 103
Which rule describes this pattern best?

_____

5. 34, 39, 33, 38, 32, 37
Which rule describes this pattern best?

_____

6. Create a number pattern in which you add 6.

_____

7. Create a number pattern in which you subtract 2, add 8.

_____

8. Create a number pattern in which you add 5, subtract 3.

_____

9. Create a number pattern in which you add 9, subtract 4.

_____

10. Create a number pattern in which you add −1, subtract 3.

_____

Think Like a Thesaurus

A thesaurus helps you choose more interesting words. See how many words you can come up with on your own, and then use a thesaurus to add more.
Try to get at least 10 synonyms for each word.

1. good

_____ _____ _____ _____ _____

_____ _____ _____ _____ _____

2. bad

_____ _____ _____ _____ _____

_____ _____ _____ _____ _____

3. pretty

_____ _____ _____ _____ _____

_____ _____ _____ _____ _____

4. big

_____ _____ _____ _____ _____

_____ _____ _____ _____ _____

Who Am I?

Unscramble the names of the famous people from U.S. history in the box. Then match them to their descriptions below. If you need help, use an encyclopedia or social studies textbook.

MASAHLLR OJHN   STUECHEM CIEFH   MAEJS AGNLO
SRSO NHJO   NRWAED OJANKSC   UAEYHQOS

1. I was the fourth chief justice of the United States, and I established the importance of the Supreme Court. I was known as the "Great Chief Justice." _____

2. I was the seventh president of the United States. I was a general in the War of 1812. My nickname was "Old Hickory." I was the founder of the modern Democratic Party.

_____

3. I worked to unite the eastern American Indian tribes into a single alliance. I joined British forces in the War of 1812. I condemned the treaty that William Henry Harrison made with the Indians. _____

4. I was a Cayuga Indian chief. I gave a speech in 1774, in which I said that I had treated the white man as my brother, but the white man had responded by killing my relatives. Thomas Jefferson was moved by my speech and wrote it down to be remembered.

_____

5. I was the chief of the Cherokee Indians from 1828 to 1866. I tried to defend Cherokee lands from white settlers. I appealed to the courts, Congress, and the president, but in the end I had to reluctantly lead my people along what became known as the "Trail of Tears." _____

6. I was the inventor of the written Cherokee language. Trees and a national park were named after me. _____

Double It

Each of the equations below have two numbers that, when removed from the equation, leave a new equation behind whose answer is exactly double the original answer. Find the numbers and write the new equation on the line.

1. 20.7 – 3.3 – 2.2 – 6.5 = 8.7 _____

2. 37.9 – 6.1 – 10.5 – 7.6 = 13.7 _____

3. 47.25 – 7.18 – 9.01 – 14.87 = 16.19 _____

4. 63.83 – 14.11 – 15.35 – 9.51 = 24.86 _____

5. 71.8 – 20.8 – 5.4 – 19.4 = 26.2 _____

6. 34.21 – 8.53 – 7.31 – 5.53 = 12.84 _____

7. 55.39 – 21.4 – 7.84 – 9.155 = 16.995 _____

8. 91.44 – 19.75 – 12.875 – 26.19 = 32.625 _____

9. 66.9 – 9.74 – 14.22 – 9.94 – 13.32 = 19.68 _____

10. 73.09 – 8.79 – 18.15 – 9.74 – 8.52 = 27.89 _____

Brooke's Budget

Brooke earns $1,100 per month from her job. The pie chart shows how Brooke spends her money. Use the chart to answer the questions below.

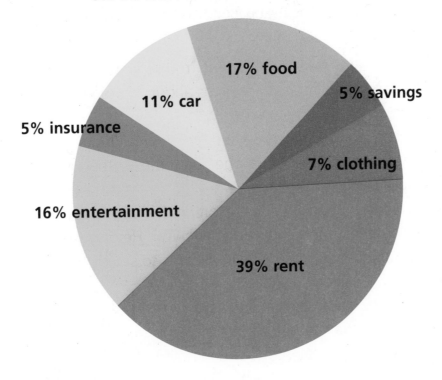

1. How much does Brooke spend on food per month? _____

2. How much does Brooke spend on clothing per month? _____

3. How much does Brooke spend on entertainment per month? _____

4. What does Brooke spend $429 on per month? _____

5. On what two things combined does Brooke spend $110 per month? _____

6. If Brooke spent $\frac{1}{2}$ as much on clothing and put that money toward her savings, how much could she save per month? _____

7. If Brooke's rent goes up 4%, how much will her rent be? _____

8. If Brooke gets a 7% raise, how much more money per month will she earn?

_____

Facts and Opinions

Sandy wrote a report on George Washington. Below is part of her report. She was supposed to include only facts about George's life. She included some opinions. Read her report and then fill out the chart on the next page to help her edit her report.

George Washington is my favorite president. You probably don't know as much about him as I do. Here are some interesting things about George Washington's life before he was a general.

George Washington was born in 1732 and grew up in Virginia. His mother's name was Mary, and his father was Augustine. George had three brothers, four half-brothers, and two sisters. Having sisters is a lot of fun.

When George was young, he liked to explore in the wilderness. This must have come in handy when he was a general in the Revolutionary War. He only went to school until he was 14 or 15. His best subject was math. Maybe he was so smart that he didn't need to finish school.

As a teenager, George became a land surveyor. At 16, he went on an expedition to the western lands for Lord Fairfax. It was his first long trip far from home. His mother must have missed him a lot. On this trip, George learned how to hunt for his own food and sleep out in the open. These are good skills to have.

George made more and more surveys for people because settlers were moving into the Shenandoah Valley. If George was out doing a survey and he saw a piece of land that he really liked, he bought it. This was smart for him to do.

In 1751, George went with his brother Lawrence to Barbados in the British West Indies. It was the only trip he ever made away from the American shores. I bet he wished he could have traveled overseas more.

George Washington

Fact	Opinion

American Indian Tribes

Circle the correct spelling for each American Indian tribe.

1. Cherokey   Cherokee   Cherrokee   Cherokie

2. Huron   Heuron   Hyuron   Huren

3. Chikasaw   Chickisaw   Chickisah   Chickasaw

4. Choctow   Choctew   Choctaw   Chactaw

5. Seminole   Seminold   Semanole   Siminole

6. Soux   Siox   Souix   Sioux

7. Chyenne   Cheyanne   Cheyenne   Cheyene

8. Arapeho   Arapaho   Arrapaho   Arappaho

9. Shawnee   Shawney   Shannee   Shawny

10. Iraqouis   Iroquis   Iroquois   Iroquoy

11. Susquehanna   Susquehana   Suschehana   Suskwehanna

12. Komanche   Comenche   Komenche   Comanche

Find the Equations

Make four true equations with three of the four numbers given for each problem. Remember that once you find one true equation you can use inverse operations to find the other correct ones.

1. 36, 7, 9, 4 _____ _____ _____ _____

2. 25, 14, 9, 11 _____ _____ _____ _____

3. 52, 9, 13, 4 _____ _____ _____ _____

4. 18, 43, 31, 12 _____ _____ _____ _____

5. 9, 6, 63, 7 _____ _____ _____ _____

6. 71, 26, 45, 55 _____ _____ _____ _____

7. 56, 7, 63, 8 _____ _____ _____ _____

8. 29, 74, 41, 33 _____ _____ _____ _____

9. 12, 38, 60, 5 _____ _____ _____ _____

10. 83, 49, 54, 34 _____ _____ _____ _____

Internet Research

Use the Internet to find the answers to these trivia questions.

1. Which state has the peach blossom for its state flower? _____

2. The Paris Peace Treaty ended the U.S. War of Independence on what date?
_____

3. How many people signed the Declaration of Independence? _____

4. What letters are NOT used to name Atlantic or Caribbean tropical storms? _____

5. In what state is the Barringer Crater located? _____

6. What are the four Galilean Satellites, and what planet do they orbit?
_____

7. The Trail of Tears was the forced relocation of Native Americans from their homelands to "Indian Territory" in which present-day state?
_____

8. What temperature is absolute zero in °C and °F? _____

Math Maze

To get through this maze you will need to follow the boxes that contain a number and an operation that could be used with another positive whole number to get an answer of 30.

Start							
5 ×	90 ÷	8 ×	37 +	14 ×	9 –	50 ÷	1 –
33 +	37 –	20 ÷	18 ÷	20 ÷	13 ×	73 +	192 +
45 ÷	3 ×	17 –	11 ×	39 +	160 ÷	26 –	0 ×
12 ×	18 +	120 ÷	21 –	2 ×	30 ÷	14 +	63 –
19 –	130 ÷	15 ×	42 –	7 +	18 ×	36 ÷	6 ×
4 ×	7 ×	72 +	90 ×	15 ÷	4 –	20 ×	60 ÷
64 +	24 –	19 ×	47 +	17 ×	55 +	11 –	29 +
27 ÷	54 +	65 ÷	13 ÷	29 –	25 ×	200 ÷	30 –

End

Different Dragons

Read the information below about two types of dragons. Then complete the Venn diagram.

Komodo Dragon

The Komodo dragon gets its name because it looks like a dragon, and it lives on Komodo Island and a few other Indonesian islands. A Komodo dragon is actually a lizard. Of course, it's a very large lizard. An adult Komodo dragon is between 6.5 and 10 feet long and usually weighs about 150 pounds. It lives in hot, dry places on the islands, but the Komodo dragon is a great swimmer. It eats other animals such as birds, monkeys, goats, deer, horses, and water buffalo. A baby Komodo dragon eats eggs, insects, and even geckoes.

Australian Water Dragon

This dragon is also a lizard. An adult will be between two and three feet long. As its name suggests, this animal lives in Australia near the water, often by lakes or rivers and is a good smimmer. Unlike the Komodo dragon, the Australian water dragon doesn't eat meat. It eats insects, worms, fish, and fruit.

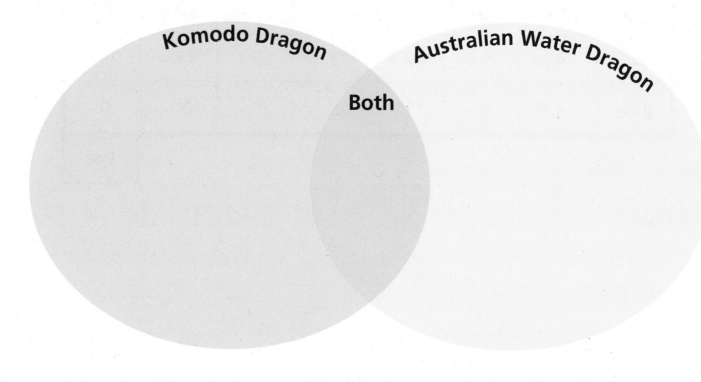

Jesse

39.84	293.54	211.8	77.65
4,532.59	45.93	4,785.43	588.72
29.39	173.55	1,088.4	295.4
183.12	65.7	6,041.05	93.51

Mindy

29.39	351.67	6,041.05	125.287
1,458.59	588.72	77.65	529.52
131.553	3,495.57	99.421	117.58
65.7	93.51	502.64	4,785.43

Marquell

83.482	93.51	520.01	99.421
1,784.68	1,940.3	4,532.59	70.012
45.93	453.11	131.553	173.55
6,041.05	1,458.59	1,088.4	3,495.57

Sandy

117.58	77.65	503.11	295.4
39.84	529.52	293.54	29.39
70.012	351.67	55.6	1,784.68
1,940.3	183.12	3,495.57	45.93

Who won?_____

Life Stories

An **autobiography** is a story you write about your own life. A **biography** is a story someone else writes about your life.

1. Write a brief autobiography about your life.

_____

_____

_____

_____

_____

2. Write a brief biography of yourself as if you were someone else writing it.

_____

_____

_____

_____

_____

Reaction Roundup

After a **chemical reaction**, a substance is changed into something different. In a **physical reaction**, the substance can change size, state, shape, or form, but the elements are not changed. Classify each change in the word bank below.

iron rusting   crushing a can   eating food   sugar dissolving in water   slicing bread
burning wood   crushing ice   a penny turning green   boiling water   cutting paper
freezing water   bending a wire   fertilizing a garden   souring milk   molding bread
salting ice on a walkway   yeast rising bread   crumpling paper
setting off fireworks   evaporating water in a puddle

Physical Reaction	Chemical Reaction

Understanding Steps

When you are giving someone directions on how to do something, sometimes it is easier to write out the steps. Other times, a diagram helps explain it better.

Think of something you know how to do. Write the steps for someone else to follow:

_____

_____

_____

_____

_____

_____

_____

Now, take those same steps. This time, draw a diagram for someone else to follow:

Test out your steps and diagram on friends and family to see which one they think is easier to follow.

The West

Fill in the letter of the year that corresponds to the events in the history of the western United States.

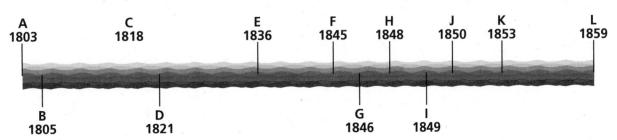

A	C		E	F	H	J	K	L
1803	1818		1836	1845	1848	1850	1853	1859

B	D	G	I
1805	1821	1846	1849

1. _____ On February 14, Oregon became the 33rd state.

2. _____ The UK and the United States agreed to a joint occupation of the Oregon region, including Washington.

3. _____ As part of the Louisiana Purchase, the United States acquired eastern Colorado.

4. _____ The United States won the Mexican–American War and acquired the western Colorado, Nevada, Arizona, New Mexico, and Utah areas from Mexico. Oregon became a territory.

5. _____ Lewis and Clark reached Washington and the Pacific Ocean.

6. _____ Oregon City was declared the territorial capital.

7. _____ Arizona became a part of Mexico.

8. _____ Congress created the Utah Territory and the Territory of New Mexico. On September 9, California became the 31st state.

9. _____ U.S. forces conquered California during the Mexican–American War.

10. _____ Texas declared its independence from Mexico. Texas became the independent Republic of Texas.

11. _____ Congress created the Washington Territory.

12. _____ On December 29, Texas became the 28th state.

Common Multiples

Write five common multiples for the numbers listed below.

1. 12, 4 _____

2. 3, 7 _____

3. 6, 18 _____

4. 2, 10 _____

5. 5, 15 _____

Now, write the least common multiple for the following numbers.

6. 8, 24 _____

7. 7, 21 _____

8. 6, 4, 5 _____

9. 3, 7, 10 _____

10. 5, 7, 9 _____

Interview Ideas

If you could interview any famous person from history, who would it be?
What kinds of questions would you ask him or her?

Famous person: _____

Five questions to ask:

1. _____

2. _____

3. _____

4. _____

5. _____

Now, use the Internet or an encyclopedia to find the information to answer those questions yourself.

1. _____
   _____

2. _____
   _____

3. _____
   _____

4. _____
   _____

5. _____
   _____

Growing Sugar Crystals

You can grow your own sugar crystals. See what happens when water evaporates from a solution of sugar water.

Here's what you'll need:
- large glass jar with a wide mouth, like a mayonnaise jar
- 4 ounces of hot water
- 8 ounces of sugar
- pencil
- piece of string or thread
- small weight

Here's what you do:

1. Pour the hot water into the jar.

2. Pour the sugar into the jar and stir it until it dissolves.

3. Tie a small weight on a piece of thread.

4. Tie the other end of the string to the middle of a pencil.

5. Hang the string and weight in the jar by placing the pencil across the jar opening.

6. Let the jar sit undisturbed for a few days.

What happens? _____

_____

_____

_____

Why it works:

The water evaporates. The sugar molecules get close together, and they form crystals.

You've made rock candy!

Distribute It!

Deacon is finishing his homework for the night. He needs help on the last section. Help Deacon use the distributive property to rewrite the problems below.

1. $5(2 + x) =$ _____

2. $7(y - 8) =$ _____

3. $10(6 + 2x) =$ _____

4. $8(4y - 9) =$ _____

5. $(3x + 4)6 =$ _____

6. $14(15 - 9y) =$ _____

7. $(7x - 1)20 =$ _____

8. $4(x + 7) + 3(4 - x) =$ _____

9. $2(y + 8) - (y - 5)5 =$ _____

10. $18(x + 3) + 13(4x - 5) =$ _____

Letter to a Character

Think of a favorite character from a book you enjoyed reading.
Follow the steps below to write that character a letter!

1. First, choose a book that has a character you like in it. _____

2. Next, choose a character in the book to write to. _____

3. Then, pick one event in the book to write about. You could tell the character what he or she did that you enjoyed. You could tell the character what you think you would have done in the same situation. _____

_____

4. Now, write your letter.

_____

_____

_____

_____

_____

_____

_____

Know Your Character

Imagine the main character of a story you'd like to write. To make your character interesting and believable, you must invent many details about him or her. Before you even start writing, you should get to know your character.

Answer the questions below to be on the road to creating a main character that will come to life on the page.

1. What is your character's name? _____

2. How old is your character? _____

3. What does your character look like? _____

_____

4. Where does your character live? _____

5. What are his or her hobbies? _____

6. What are his or her accomplishments? _____

7. What makes your character happy? _____

8. What makes your character sad? _____

9. Who are your character's close friends and family? _____

_____

10. Other details _____

_____

Thank-You Cards

It's the second-to-last week of school and the students want to make thank-you cards for all of their teachers. They have one week to finish them so that they can give them to their teachers during the last week. The chart below shows the days on which the students made cards for specific teachers. Use the chart to help you answer the questions on the next page.

	Monday	Tuesday	Wednesday	Thursday	Friday	Saturday	Sunday
Henry	Mrs. Paulis, Mr. Klein, Mr. Chase	none	Mrs. Martin	Mr. Mitchell, Mrs. Lasalle	Mrs. Ellington	Mrs. Allen, Mr. Tripp, Mr. Ferns, Mrs. Smith	Mr. Mendez, Mrs. King, Mr. Gregory
Delilah	none	Mrs. Martin, Mrs. Allen, Mrs. Smith, Mr. Gregory	Mr. Chase, Mr. Mitchell, Mrs. Lasalle	none	Mrs. Ellington, Mr. Tripp	Mrs. Paulis, Mr. Mendez	Mr. Klein, Mr. Ferns, Mrs. King
Ken	Mrs. Ellington, Mr. Tripp, Mr. Ferns, Mr. Gregory	none	none	Mrs. Paulis, Mrs. Martin, Mr. Mendez, Mrs. King	Mr. Klein, Mrs. Allen	Mrs. Lasalle, Mrs. Smith	Mr. Chase, Mr. Mitchell
Suzanne	Mr. Mitchell, Mr. Mendez	Mrs. Paulis	Mr. Klein, Mr. Chase, Mrs. King	Mrs. Ellington, Mr. Tripp, Mr. Ferns	Mrs. Martin, Mrs. Lasalle, Mrs. Allen, Mrs. Smith, Mr. Gregory	none	none
Tim	Mr. Chase	Mrs. Paulis, Mrs. Lasalle, Mrs. King	Mr. Mitchell, Mr. Ferns, Mr. Mendez	Mrs. Allen, Mrs. Smith, Mr. Gregory	Mrs. Ellington	Mr. Klein, Mr. Tripp	Mrs. Martin
Ashlee	none	Mr. Mitchell, Mr. Tripp, Mr. Ferns, Mrs. Smith, Mr. Gregory	none	Mr. Chase, Mrs. Martin, Mrs. Ellington	Mrs. Lasalle	Mrs. Paulis, Mr. Klein, Mrs. Allen, Mr. Mendez, Mrs. King	none
Walter	Mrs. Lasalle, Mrs. Ellington, Mrs. Smith	Mr. Klein, Mrs. Martin, Mr. Mendez	Mr. Chase, Mr. Tripp, Mrs. King, Mr. Gregory	none	Mrs. Paulis, Mrs. Allen, Mr. Ferns	none	Mr. Mitchell

1. Who finished Mr. Tripp's card first? _____

2. Which student made the most cards in the first two days? _____

3. Which student made the most cards over the weekend? _____

4. Which student finished all of the male teachers' cards first? _____

5. Which student finished all of the cards first? _____

6. Who was the last student to finish Mrs. Martin's card?_____

Now create your own thank-you card. Think of a person to whom you would like to show gratitude. Then draw the front and inside of the card. Don't forget to write why you are thanking him or her.

front inside

Figurative Language

Figurative language makes writing more colorful and descriptive.
You can use figurative language in your own writing.

A **simile** compares two things using the words *like* or *as*.
Example: Her hair is <u>as soft as silk</u>.

A **metaphor** compares two things without using *like* or *as*.
Example: The sun was <u>a warm blanket</u> on my back.

Personification gives animals or objects human qualities.
Example: The trees <u>stretched out their arms to wave</u> to me.

Alliteration repeats the same consonant sound at the beginnings of words.
Example: The <u>d</u>aisies were <u>d</u>ancing in the <u>d</u>ew-<u>d</u>renched <u>d</u>aylight.

Onomatopoeia uses words that imitate the sounds they make.
Example: The birds <u>chirped</u> as we walked by their nest.

Now, take the beginning of each sentence and see if you can complete it five times using the kind of language indicated. Use your imagination!

1. The big bumblebee…

Simile: _____

Metaphor: _____

Personification: _____

Alliteration: _____

Onomatopoeia: _____

2. The cool wind…

Simile: _____

Metaphor: _____

Personification: _____

Alliteration: _____

Onomatopoeia: _____

3. The shy squirrel…

Simile: _____

Metaphor: _____

Personification: _____

Alliteration: _____

Onomatopoeia: _____

4. The tall trees…

Simile: _____

Metaphor: _____

Personification: _____

Alliteration: _____

Onomatopoeia: _____

5. The curious cat…

Simile: _____

Metaphor: _____

Personification: _____

Alliteration: _____

Onomatopoeia: _____

6. The old house…

Simile: _____

Metaphor: _____

Personification: _____

Alliteration: _____

Onomatopoeia: _____

107

Acids and Bases

Acids taste sour, corrode metals, and turn litmus paper red.
Bases feel slippery and turn litmus paper blue.

Classify the items in the word bank below as an *acid*, a *base*, or *neutral*. Use litmus paper if you have it, or use the Internet to help you.

lemon juice	vinegar	ammonia	milk
orange juice	tea	water	grapefruit juice
toothpaste	baking soda	soda	soap

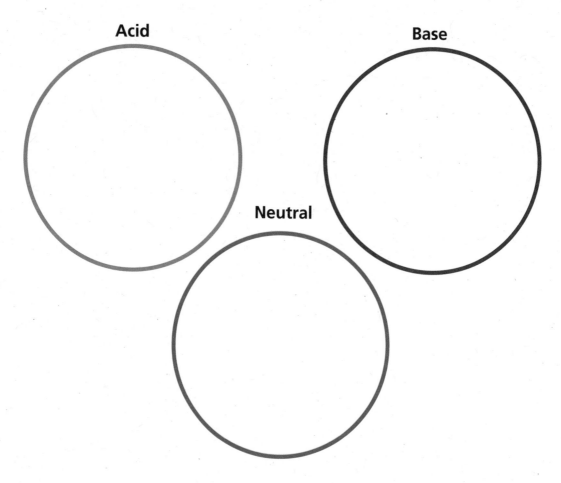

Acid

Base

Neutral

What other acids and bases can you come up with? _____

_____

Missing Exponents

All of the numbers below have lost their exponents. Use the answers to figure out the missing exponents, and then fill them in. Remember, an exponent is used to signify repeated multiplication.

For example: $4 \times 4 \times 4 = 4^3$

(Hint: Try seeing how many times you can divide the base number into the answer until your answer is the base number.)

1. 5 ☐ = 25

2. 7 ☐ = 2,401

3. 9 ☐ = 59,049

4. 2 ☐ = 256

5. 4 ☐ = 64

6. 10 ☐ = 100,000

7. 3 ☐ = 27

8. 12 ☐ = 144

9. 13 ☐ = 28,561

10. 6 ☐ = 279,936

Precise Words

Dion was writing a story about what happens in his backyard. He wrote this sentence:

Two squirrels <u>move</u> from limb to limb in the tree.

He was trying to show the reader how fast and playful the squirrels were. Dion made this word map to pick a better word to use than *move*.

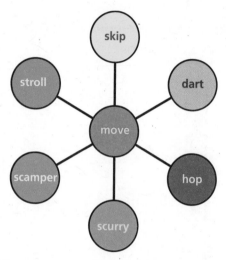

He saw that there were a few words that he could use:
Two squirrels <u>scamper</u> from limb to limb in the tree.
Two squirrels <u>scurry</u> from limb to limb in the tree.
Two squirrels <u>hop</u> from limb to limb in the tree.

All of these choices make the sentence more vivid.

You can use a word map to find more precise, vivid words to use in your writing. Make a word map for each underlined word. Then rewrite the sentence using the best word from your word map.

1. I had a <u>nice</u> vacation.

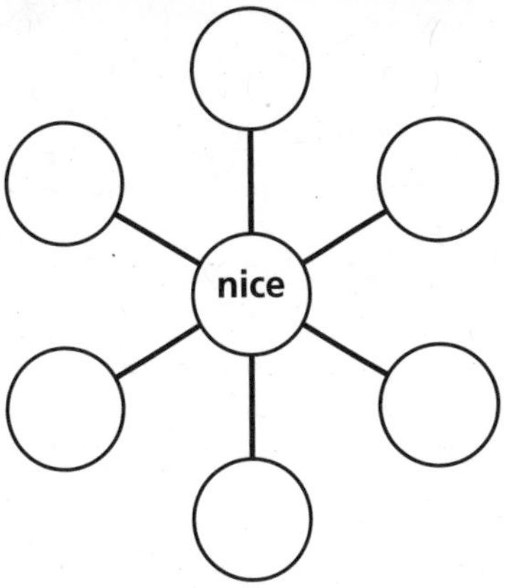

_____

_____

_____

_____

2. The <u>small</u> kitten was sleeping.

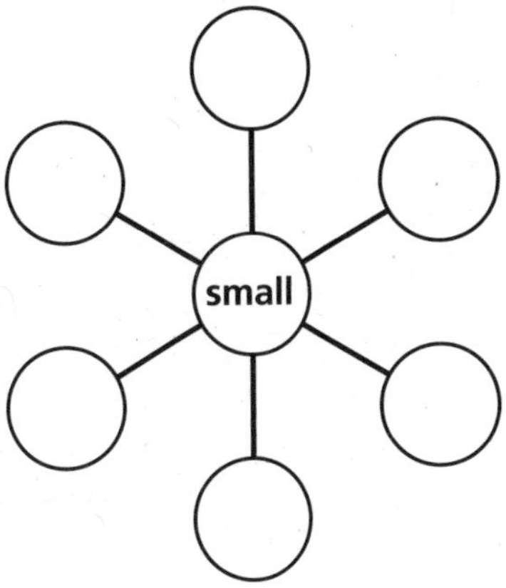

_____

_____

_____

_____

3. We sat in the <u>hot</u> sun.

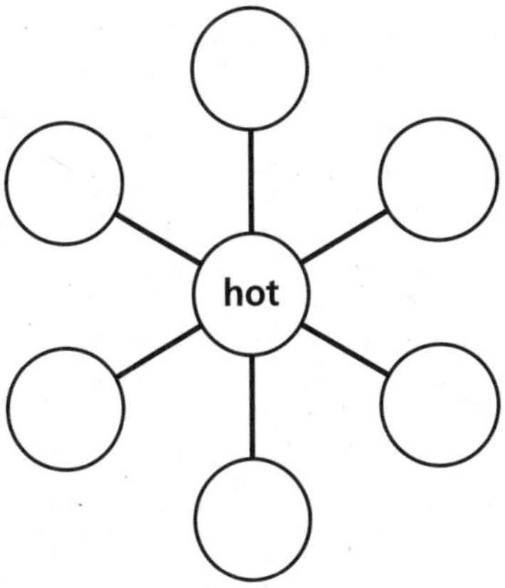

_____

_____

_____

_____

4. The sky was a <u>bright</u> blue.

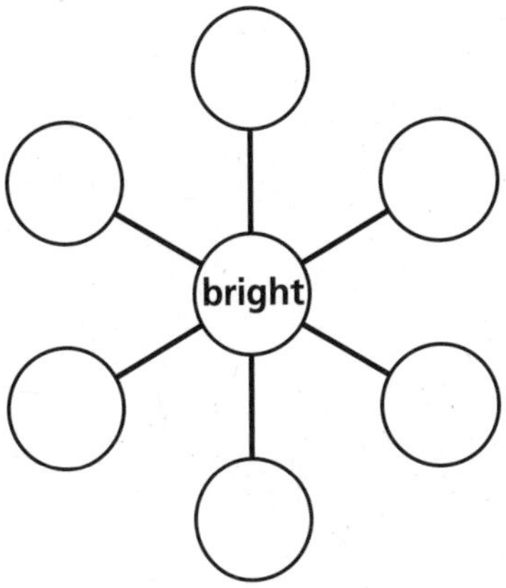

_____

_____

_____

_____

Declaration of Independence

Complete this crossword puzzle about the Declaration of Independence.

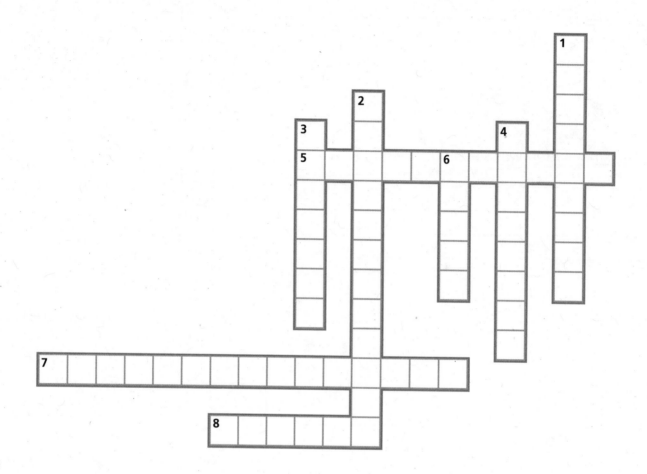

Across

5. "they are endowed by their Creator with certain _____ rights"

7. _____ _____ drafted the Declaration of Independence.

8. the nickname for those who remained loyal to the king

Down

1. the works of this English philosopher were drawn upon to write the Declaration of Independence

2. treaty that ended the French and Indian War in 1763

3. "Life, Liberty, and the _____ of Happiness"

4. the nickname for those who opposed the king

6. "All men are created _____."

Shipshape

Draw a line to match each shape to its description.

A pentagon is a five-sided polygon.

An isosceles triangle has two sides of equal length.

A quadrilateral is a four-sided polygon.

A hexagon is a six-sided polygon.

An equilateral triangle has three sides of equal length.

A scalene triangle has three sides of different lengths.

A right triangle has one right angle.

A rectangle is a four-sided polygon with four right angles.

Atomic Structure

An atom is the smallest unit of matter with properties of a particular element.
Unscramble each term relating to atoms to complete the sentences.

1. The center of an atom is its (luncuse) _____.

2. The part of the nucleus with a positive charge is the (tnorop) _____.

3. Parts of the atom have a positive, negative, or neutral (rgheac) _____.

4. Protons and neutrons are made of tiny particles called (rkusaq) _____.

5. The (oruentn) _____ is the part of the nucleus with neither a negative nor a positive charge.

6. An (rneolcte) _____ orbits the nucleus and has a negative charge.

7. A (ecmlouel) _____ is made up of two or more atoms.

8. A (eynaivgelt) _____ charged atom has more electrons than protons.

Writing Challenge

Write a story that includes all of the words in the word bank. Make sure to give your story a title.

hippopotamus	teleportation	warehouse	gravity
molasses	disguise	certificate	journal

_____

by _____

_____

_____

_____

_____

_____

_____

_____

_____

Acrostic Poems

An acrostic poem is another form of free-verse poetry. Each line begins with a letter from the title. Sometimes each line has only one word. Other times, the number of words in each line varies.

Here is an example of an acrostic poem:

Flowers
Fragrant
lovely
often
wilting
enjoy
rose
scents

Write your own acrostic poems.

Summer

S_____

U_____

M_____

M_____

E_____

R_____

Recess

R_____

E_____

C_____

E_____

S_____

S_____

Family

F_____

A_____

M_____

I_____

L_____

Y_____

Your Name: _____

_____

_____

_____

_____

_____

_____

Simplifying Expressions

Write equations for each problem below and then find the answer.

1. One day a student read 6 pages before going to bed. The next 3 nights, she read 4 pages each night. The following night, she read 7 pages. How many pages did she read in all?

_____

2. It snowed 4 inches 2 days in a row. The next day, it snowed 5 inches. Then, the following 3 days, it snowed 3 inches each day. How many inches did it snow in total? _____

3. There were 2 dogs being walked in a park. An hour later, 3 more dogs came into the park. The next hour, 1 dog came and 2 dogs left. The next hour, $\frac{1}{4}$ the number of dogs in the park left. How many dogs are left in the park now? _____

4. Phillip is 4 years old. His older sister is 5 years older than him. His cousin is $\frac{1}{3}$ older than Phillip's older sister. Phillip's mom is 3 times older than his cousin. How old is Phillip's mom?

_____

5. Gillian named 3 trees in the park. The next week, she named 4 more trees. The next week, she named 2 times the number of trees she named the week before. The next 2 weeks, she named 6 trees each week. How many trees did Gillian name? _____

6. Skip weighs twice as much as Sly does. Sly weighs 3 more pounds than Spike. Spike weighs $\frac{1}{3}$ of the weight of Tito. Tito weighs 27 pounds. How much does Skip weigh?

_____

7. There were 8 people on a bus. At the first stop, $\frac{1}{2}$ the number of people on the bus got on. At the next stop, 5 people got on. At the next two stops, 3 people got off the bus at each stop. At the next stop, 2 more people got on. How many people are on the bus now?

_____

8. Yolanda collected 18 cans to recycle in January. The next two months, she collected 20 cans each month. The month after that, she collected $\frac{1}{2}$ the amount of cans she had collected for the year so far. The following month, she collected 12 more cans. How many cans did Yolanda collect in total? _____

Super Sally

Draw a line to match each cause to its effect.

Cause

Sally's basketball team won its game.

Sally woke up late for school.

Sally forgot her lunch.

Sally got the highest score on the math test.

Sally brought her books back to the library late.

Sally went to the grocery store with her mom.

Sally helped her mom with the dishes.

Sally finished the book she was reading.

Sally dropped her ice-cream cone on the floor.

Sally set her alarm.

Effect

Sally had to buy school lunch.

Sally cleaned ice cream off the floor.

Sally woke up on time for school.

Sally got a trophy.

Sally started a new book.

Sally helped choose what to have for dinner.

Sally missed her bus.

Sally earned extra allowance.

Sally's teacher gave her a gold star.

Sally paid a late fee at the library.

Compound Words

You can combine words to make **compound words**. Match each word from the first column with a word from the second column to create a compound word. Then write each compound word below. Be careful! Some words might have more than one match. You have to choose the right matches so that every word has a match.

barn	apple
bed	board
black	cast
broad	graph
dough	man
fore	mare
gang	name
hard	nut
lime	plank
live	ship
nick	smith
night	stock
photo	stone
pine	time
star	ward
west	yard

_____

_____

_____

_____

_____

_____

_____

_____

_____

_____

_____

_____

_____

_____

_____

_____

Circle Graphs

The student government at Sunnybrook Middle School has done a few surveys to find out some information about the students. The data was made into circle graphs so that it would be easier to analyze. Answer the questions about the graphs below.

Favorite Lunch Food

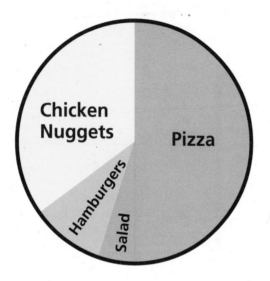

Least Favorite Lunch Food

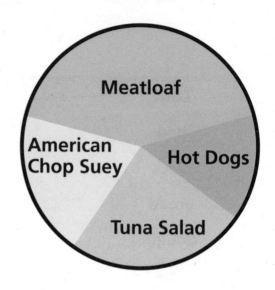

Favorite School Color

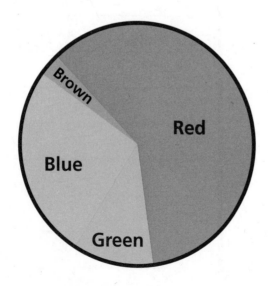

Favorite School Mascot

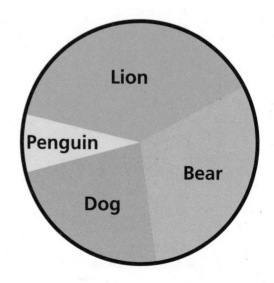

1. Which school mascot do students like the least? _____

2. Which food is the second most favorite? _____

3. Which two animals look about tied for favorite school mascot? _____

4. Which color is liked by about half as many people as blue? _____

5. What is the second most disliked food? _____

6. Which color do more than half of the students surveyed prefer? _____

7. Which two animals combined are liked about as much as the lion? _____

8. Out of all of the graphs, which item got the least number of votes? _____

For an extra challenge, take a poll of your friends or family.
Tally the information and draw your own circle graph below.

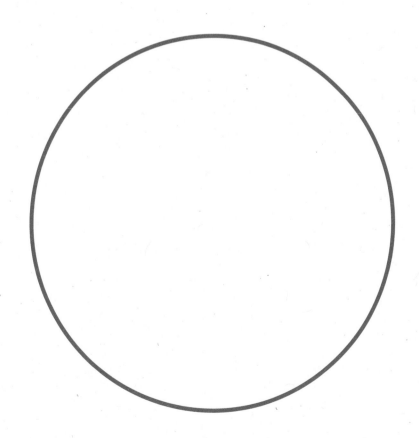

Mixed-Up Fairy Tales

Choose your favorite fairy tale, folk tale, fable, or nursery rhyme. Retell the story from the point of view of one of the characters. For example, you could tell "Little Red Riding Hood" from the wolf's point of view.

Story chosen: _____

_____

_____

_____

_____

_____

_____

_____

_____

_____

How is the story you wrote different from the original story?

_____

_____

Citizenship Test

If you were trying to become a U.S. citizen, you would have to take a citizenship test. These are some questions that you could be asked. Time yourself to see how many minutes it takes for you to answer these questions. Then check the answer key to see how many of your answers are correct.

1. How many stars are on the U.S. flag? _____

2. What color are the stars on the flag? _____

3. What do the stars on the flag stand for? _____

4. How many stripes are on the flag? _____

5. What color are the stripes? _____

6. What do the stripes stand for? _____

7. What day is Independence Day? _____

8. What country did we fight for our independence? _____

9. Who was our first president? _____

10. What year was the Constitution written? _____

11. Who said, "Give me Liberty or give me Death"? _____

12. What is the national anthem? _____

_____minutes

_____correct

Exploring English Etymology

Etymology is the history of a word. The English language is constantly changing.
Here are five ways that we get new words.

Borrowed words: Many words come from foreign languages. For example, *toboggan* was a Native American word.

Words from people and places: Other words were the names of people or places. For example, *frankfurter* comes from Frankfurt, Germany.

Words from sounds: There are words that imitate sounds they describe, for example, *moo* or *hoot*.

Words shortened from longer words: We shorten words to make them easier to spell and say, the way we give a person a nickname. For example, the word *bus* is a shortened form of *omnibus*.

Words made by joining two other words: Compound words are created from joining two words, for example, *bookcase*. A blend is a compound word with letters dropped. For example, *smog* is a blend of *smoke* and *fog*.

Use a dictionary to look up each word's etymology. Write which category it falls into: *borrowed*, *name of a person*, *name of a place*, *sounds*, *shortened*, *compound*, or *blend*.

1. mike _____

2. snowshoe _____

3. giggle _____

4. pop _____

5. gas _____

6. burro _____

7. scrooge _____

8. motel _____

Challenge: snowmobile _____

Sudoku

Fill in the grid so that every row, every column, and every
3 x 3 box contains the numbers 1 through 9.

9	3			5	4	7		8
8		7		2		3	4	6
4								9
				1		6	8	7
3			8	6			5	2
	8	1	5		2	9	3	4
2		5	3			4	9	1
	4			9	6		7	
			1		5			3

Misleading Advertisements

Sometimes ads make promises they can't keep so that you will buy what they are selling. See the example below, then explain how each of the product claims make unrealistic promises.

For example:
The cereal can't really help you get As. It won't make you smarter.

1. Wear Speedy Sneakers and you'll win every race!

_____

2. Put Salon Spritz in your hair and you'll look like a movie star!

_____

3. Drink Cool Cola and you'll have lots of friends!

_____

4. Use Tub Scrubbers and you'll never have to wash your bathtub again!

_____

5. Buy the Perfect Pillow and you'll never want to get out of bed!

_____

6. Wash your floor with Wonder Wax and you can eat off it!

_____

Come up with your own unrealistic promises for some products you use.

Solids, Liquids, and Gases!

There are different states in which matter can exist. For example, very cold water turns into ice, which is water in a solid state. Water can also be a liquid, as in the case of drinking water. When water is heated, it turns into steam, which is a gas. Classify each item in the box according to its state at room temperature. Then add some of your own items to each category.

| gasoline | iron | alcohol | wax | water | paper |
| olive oil | oxygen | steam | snow | helium | sugar |

Solids	Liquids	Gases

Expository Essays on European Explorers

Expository writing is a type of writing that provides a lot of detailed information in order to teach the reader about a certain subject. In an expository essay, you write detailed descriptions and discussions about a topic. Follow the steps below to write an expository essay.

1. Choose one of the European explorers below. Circle his name.

Christopher Columbus   Francisco Vásquez de Coronado

Henry Hudson   Jacques Cartier

2. List three sources you can go to for information.

_____

3. Use the sources to fill in the graphic organizer.

A. Who was he?
B. Where was he from?
C. When did he live?
D. Where did he explore?
E. Why is he important to remember?
F. How did others feel about him?

4. Now use the details you found to write a short essay on a separate piece of paper.

More Sudoku

Fill in the grid so that every row, every column, and every
3 x 3 box contains the numbers 1 through 9.

	4		1	7	3			
6								
			8	6		3	5	4
2	7	8		5				
	9	3	7	1		5	8	
	2	1	9				4	5
7						2	9	8

Great Plains Peoples

Fill in the Venn diagram below about the people of the Great Plains.
Use the words in the word bank for help.

lived in lodges   nomads   carried their belongings on travois
Pawnee Indians   farmers   lived in villages   hunted buffalo
Lakota Indians   Omaha Indians   followed herds of buffalo

Western Plains Indians   **Eastern Plains Indians**

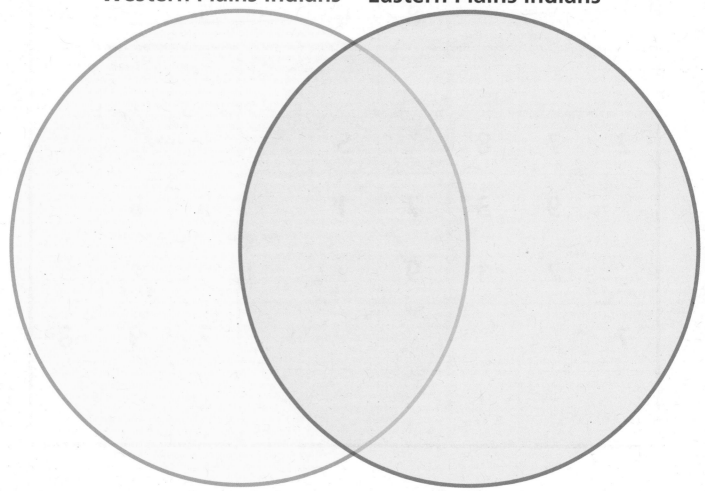

Cross Sums

Place a number from 1 to 9 in each white box without repeating a number in any sum. The yellow boxes have hints. The number below a diagonal line is the sum of the numbers going down. The number above a diagonal line is the sum of the numbers going right.
The first one has been done for you.

Monkeying Around

Read the passage below about monkeys. Use what you learn to complete the Venn diagram.

Monkeys

Monkeys are mammals. They are in the same order as humans and apes, called *primates*. Monkeys are typically found in the tropical regions of Africa, Asia, Central America, and South America.

Scientists categorize monkeys into two groups: Old World monkeys and New World monkeys. Old World monkeys live in Africa and Asia. New World monkeys are from Central America and South America. They are different in many ways.

The nostrils in New World monkeys are spaced widely apart, while the Old World monkeys have nostrils that are close together. Old World monkeys have 32 teeth, like humans, while New World monkeys have 36 teeth. No Old World monkey can grasp things with its tail, but some New World monkeys can. All monkeys have long arms and legs to help them leap, climb, and run. They can use their hands and feet to hold on to things, like tree branches.

All New World monkeys live in trees. Some Old World monkeys live in trees, but others live on the ground. Even the monkeys who live on the ground descended from monkeys who lived in trees. So, all monkeys' bodies are mainly suited for moving through trees. Many Old World monkeys have cheek pouches, like a squirrel, that let them store food. No New World monkey has this pouch.

Old World monkeys have opposable thumbs that let them grasp small pieces of food. Humans also have opposable thumbs; it's how we can hold things. Most New World monkeys have only partially opposable thumbs that can't move as freely as Old World monkeys' thumbs.

All monkeys live in groups. New World monkeys rarely have more than 20 members in a group, but Old World monkey groups can have 30 to 100 members.

While monkeys have many differences, they are all intelligent animals that can adapt to a huge range of different environments.

Now complete this Venn diagram about Old World monkeys and New World monkeys.

Old World Monkeys   **New World Monkeys**

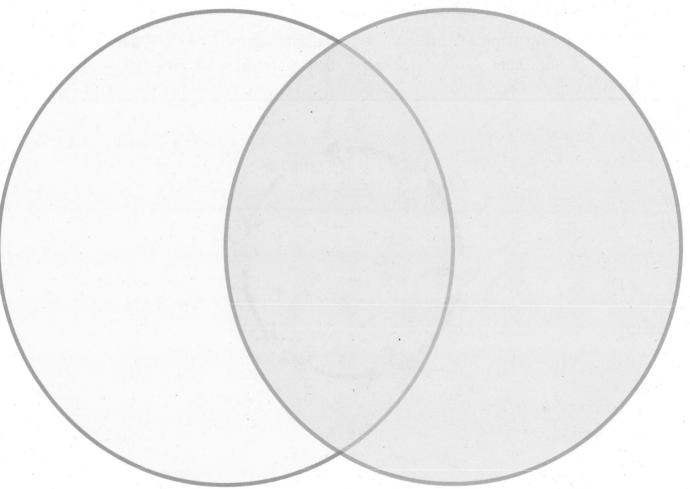

State Changes

Matter can change from one state to another. Put each of the items in the word bank into the correct category below.

cooling magma   melting ice   freezing water   morning dew
humidifier   rain   dry ice   boiling water   dehumidifier

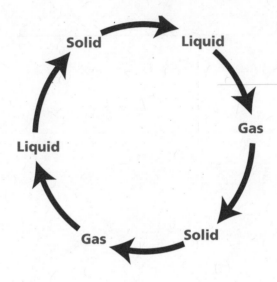

Solid → Liquid → Gas → Solid → Gas → Liquid

Solid to liquid

_____

_____

_____

Liquid to gas

_____

_____

_____

Gas to solid

_____

_____

_____

Solid to gas

_____

_____

_____

Gas to liquid

_____

_____

_____

Liquid to solid

_____

_____

_____

Road Rules

Read the facts about Emmett's road trip. Then use them to answer the questions.

Emmett lives in Appleton. He will be driving though all of these towns on the same road:

Mountville is 230.7 miles farther than Junction.
Chaney is 75.5 miles farther than Mountville.
Sun City is 56.2 miles closer than Junction.
Danville is 83.6 miles farther than Sun City.
Faith is 36.8 miles closer than Sun City.
Junction is 102.3 miles from Emmett's home in Appleton.

1. Write the city names in order, from closest to farthest from Appleton.

_____

2. How many miles is it from Junction to Chaney? _____

3. How many miles is it from Mountville to Faith? _____

4. How many miles is it from Sun City to Danville? _____

5. Emmet drove from Danville to Chaney. Then he drove back to Sun City. How many miles did he drive? _____

Pros and Cons

In every discussion or debate, there are two sides. The pro side is in favor of the issue. The con side is against the issue. No matter which side of an issue your opinion is, it is important to be able to see the other side's opinion. For each issue below, write one statement in favor of the issue and one statement against the issue.

1. Schools should serve only healthy snacks.

Pro: _____

_____

Con: _____

_____

2. Everyone should have a pet.

Pro: _____

_____

Con: _____

_____

3. School should be open year-round.

Pro: _____

_____

Con: _____

_____

4. Teachers should not assign homework.

Pro: _____

_____

Con: _____

_____

5. Kids shouldn't watch TV.

Pro: _____

_____

Con: _____

_____

6. Everyone should have a garden.

Pro: _____

_____

Con: _____

_____

7. Kids shouldn't play video games.

Pro: _____

_____

Con: _____

_____

Convince Me!

Look at the statements you wrote on the previous page. Choose one issue and one side. If you had to persuade someone from the other side to agree with you, how would you do it? Write a paragraph explaining your side of the issue. Be sure to consider the other side's opinion.

_____

_____

_____

_____

_____

_____

_____

_____

_____

_____

_____

Hidato Maze

Fill in the missing numbers 1 to 25 to discover the hidden path within the grid.
Use consecutive numbers that connect horizontally, vertically, or diagonally to win.

		Start 1	18	
	4			19
8		3		
	9			23
11		25 End		

Big Budget

Ada just got her first apartment. It's time to start budgeting. Her job as a veterinary assistant pays $25,000 a year. To make sure she has enough money, Ada has written out her yearly budget in percentages.

Write out Ada's yearly budget in dollar amounts.

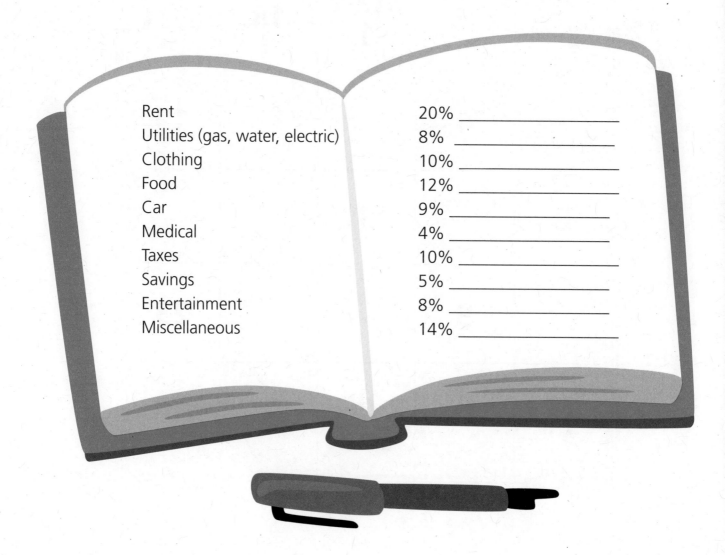

Rent — 20% _____

Utilities (gas, water, electric) — 8% _____

Clothing — 10% _____

Food — 12% _____

Car — 9% _____

Medical — 4% _____

Taxes — 10% _____

Savings — 5% _____

Entertainment — 8% _____

Miscellaneous — 14% _____

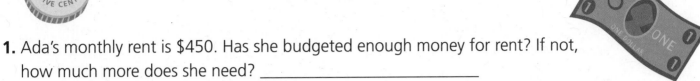

Use Ada's budget to answer the questions.

1. Ada's monthly rent is $450. Has she budgeted enough money for rent? If not, how much more does she need? _____

2. Ada reduced her clothing budget by 2%. How much more money will she have in her overall budget now? Can she afford her rent with the money she saved on clothes?

_____

3. Ada sold her car. She will now put half the money she planned to spend on car expenses into savings. The other half will go toward miscellaneous items. How much will she add to savings? _____
How much total money will now be set aside for miscellaneous items? _____

4. Ada wants to reduce her entertainment budget by 3%. How much money will she have left for entertainment? _____

5. Ada needs to add 2.5% to her budget to cover rising utility costs. How much less will she have in her budget? _____

Opposites Attract

Some words can be changed into their antonyms by only changing their prefix or suffix. For example, the words *inside* and *outside*. Change the prefixes or suffixes for the words below. If the new word is the original word's antonym, then write it on the line. If it is not the antonym (or not a word), then write "not the antonym."

1. inflate _____

2. overpass _____

3. underneath _____

4. colorful _____

5. decide _____

6. hairless _____

Can you come up with any of your own pairs that work?

_____   _____

_____   _____

_____   _____

_____   _____

The Respiratory System

Put the statements below in order from 1 through 8 to show the order in which things occur in the respiratory system.

_____ Air passes through the cilia, which keep dirt and mucus out of the lungs.

_____ Air flows through the bronchial tubes to enter the lungs.

_____ Carbon dioxide enters the alveoli and leaves the body.

_____ Air passes through smaller tubes, called bronchioles, in the lungs to reach the alveoli, or air sacs.

_____ Oxygen passes into red blood cells in blood vessels.

_____ Air goes down the trachea, or windpipe.

_____Air enters the nose.

_____The diaphragm contracts and the lungs expand.

Your lungs contain almost 1,500 miles of airways, 300,000 bronchioles, and more than 300 million alveoli!

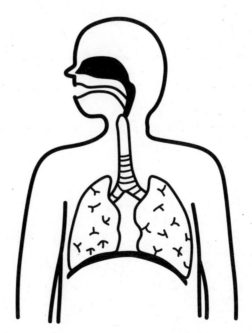

Back to Your Roots

Knowing common Latin and Greek roots will help you figure out the meaning of words you don't know. Match each root in the word bank to its meaning.

aud	bibl	fin	ject	man	meter	ped	photo
	port	spec, spic, scope		struct	vid, vis		

1. to hear _____

2. to see or look _____

3. to carry _____

4. to see or look _____

5. to build _____

6. hand _____

7. to throw _____

8. feet _____

9. book _____

10. end _____

11. to measure _____

12. light _____

For an extra challenge, see if you can think of five words for each root. Check your answers in a dictionary.

Food for Thought

Solve the riddle below by writing the letter that goes with each ordered pair on the line.

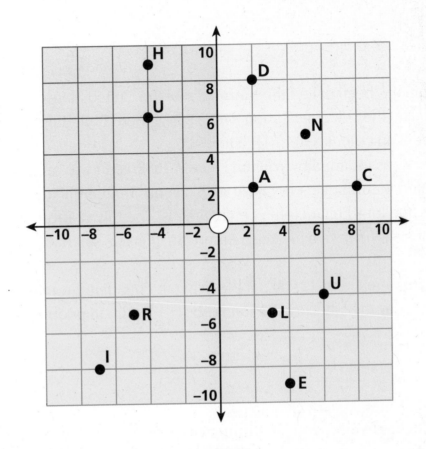

What two things can you never eat for breakfast?

___ ___ ___ ___ ___

(3,−5)   (−4,6)   (5,5)   (8,2)   (−4,9)

___ ___ ___

(2,2)   (5,5)   (2,8)

___ ___ ___ ___ ___ ___

(2,8)   (−7,−8)   (5,5)   (5,5)   (4,−9)   (−5,−5)

Look Closely

The following readings may appear to be identical, but 10 changes have been made to the second one. Circle the changes in the second reading.

Reading 1

Philadelphia has been called the birthplace of the United States. Both the Declaration of Independence and the U.S. Constitution were signed there. Philadelphia also served as the capital of the American colonies from 1775 to 1783.

Philadelphia was founded by William Penn in 1682. Penn was an English Quaker who was persecuted for his beliefs. Because of this, Penn wanted Philadelphia to be a place of religious freedom. Philadelphia's nickname is "The City of Brotherly Love" because *philadelphia* means *brotherly love* in Greek. American Quakers still have their headquarters there.

In 1790, there were about 42,000 people living in Philadelphia, making it the largest city in the nation. Today the city's population is about 1.5 million people. It is the largest city in Pennsylvania.

Reading 2

Philadelphia has been called the birthplace of the United States. Neither the Declaration of Independence and the U.S. Constitution were signed there. Philadelphia also served as the capital of the American colonies from 1776 to 1782.

Philadelphia was founded by William Penn in 1582. Penn was a French Quaker who was persecuted for his beliefs. Because of this, Penn never wanted Philadelphia to be a place of religious freedom. Philadelphia's nickname is "The City of Brotherly Love" because *pennsylvania* means *brotherly love* in Latin. American Quakers still have their headquarters there.

In 1790, there were about 42,000 people living in Philadelphia, making it the second largest city in the nation. Today the city's population is about 1.5 million. It is the largest city in Pennsylvania.

Prime Factorization

Use prime factorization to solve the problems below.

$$96 \div 2 = 48$$
$$48 \div 2 = 24$$
$$24 \div 2 = 12$$
$$12 \div 2 = 6$$
$$6 \div 2 = 3$$
$$3 \div 3 = 1$$
$$96 = 2 \times 2 \times 2 \times 2 \times 2 \times 3$$

1. Which number between 15 and 20 has all 2s as its prime factors? _____

2. Liz's lucky number is a prime number between 30 and 35. What is her lucky number? _____

3. Which numbers between 2 and 50 have 11 in their prime factorization? _____

4. Which numbers between 2 and 50 have 13 in their prime factorization? _____

5. Which numbers between 2 and 10 do NOT have a 2 in their prime factorization? _____

6. Which number between 40 and 45 has 7 as one of its prime factors? _____

7. What two sets of five consecutive numbers between 2 and 50 are not prime numbers? _____

8. What two numbers between 2 and 50 have three different numbers in their prime factorizations? _____

Keep to the Topic

When you are writing expository paragraphs, you should only write details that are important to the main idea. The students who wrote the expository paragraphs below have gone off topic. Cross out the sentences that are unnecessary.

1. Mountains are landforms that are a lot higher than the land around them. My mother says that I make mountains out of molehills. The climate gets colder and wetter the higher you go on a mountain. I'm afraid of heights. You can find mountains on land as well as in the sea. In fact, the world's longest system of mountains is almost completely underwater!

2. Vegetables or fruit that are preserved in vinegar are called pickles. The most common vegetable used is the cucumber. But you can also use cabbage, carrots, olives, peaches, peppers, or tomatoes. My cousin is allergic to tomatoes. First, you soak the vegetable in brine, which is salty water. The ocean has lots of salty water. Then an acid is added, or it can be created by bacteria through fermentation. We learned about acids in science class. The pickles are then flavored with seasonings.

3. A cricket is a jumping insect. It is related to the grasshopper. Do you remember that cricket from *Pinocchio*? He wore clothes. Crickets make songs by rubbing their two front wings together. They hear the songs with organs that are in their front legs. Every kind of cricket has a unique song, and the males usually produce them. In my family, my mother is the best singer. The songs help the males and females find each other. I don't like to get lost.

4. Candles have been around for a long time. They are made from wax and burned to give light. My parents like to have dinner by candlelight. The flame melts the wax and helps it burn. I like blowing out the candles on my birthday cake. You can make a candle by hand by dipping a wick over and over into liquid wax. You can also pour liquid wax into a mold with a suspended wick. A third way is to roll sheets of soft wax around a wick. Lots of people make candles as a hobby. My hobby is stamp collecting.

Cause

Effect

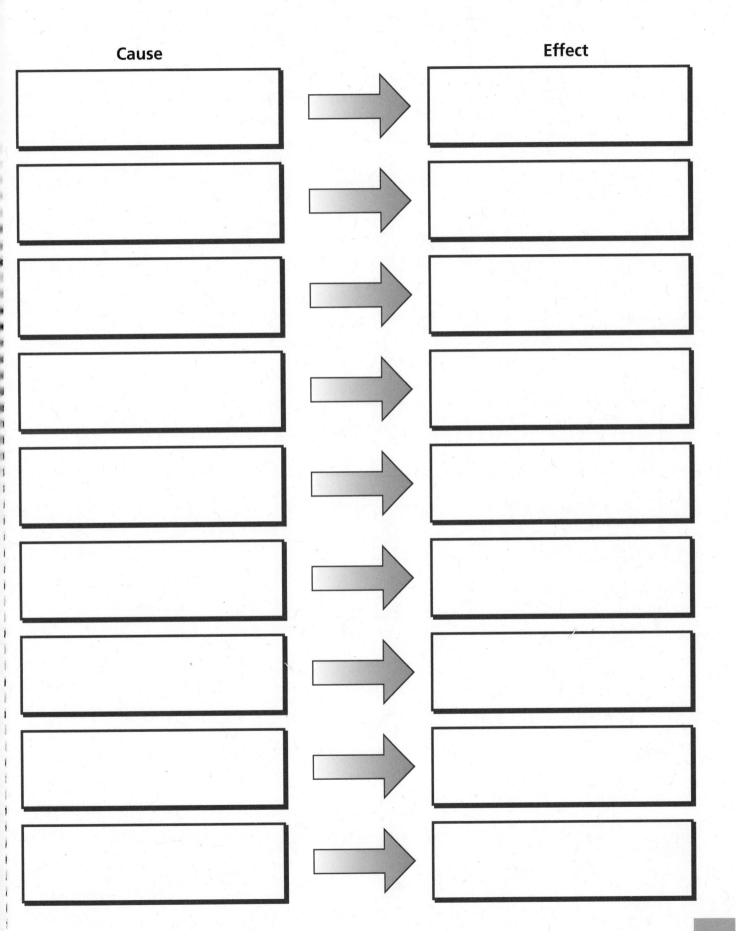

Mean Scores

Aaron, Bobby, Cameron, Darren, and Eric all received different scores on their math tests. The scores were 75, 80, 85, 90, and 95. Use the clues below to find who got which score. Then mark the chart with Xs to show the boys' scores.

Clues:

1. The average of Aaron's and Bobby's scores is 80.

2. The average of Bobby's and Cameron's scores is 82.5.

3. The average of Cameron's and Darren's scores is 85.

4. The average of Darren's and Eric's scores is 87.5.

5. The average of Bobby's and Darren's scores is 77.5.

	75	80	85	90	95
Aaron					
Bobby					
Cameron					
Darren					
Eric					

Name That Number

Read the clues to find the correct number.

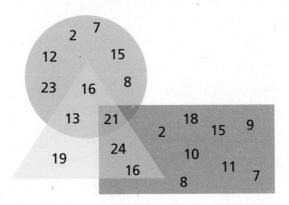

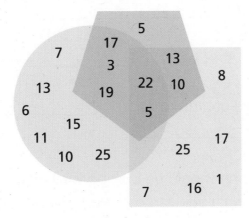

1. It is not an even number. It is in the rectangle and the triangle. It is more than 13. What is the number?

_____

2. It is an odd number. It is in the circle and the triangle. The numbers in its ones and tens place add up to 4. What is the number? _____

3. It is an even number. It is not in the pentagon. It is divisible by 3. What is the number? _____

4. It is an odd number. It is in the circle. It is divisible by 5. It is not 25. What is the number? _____

Roger's Research

Roger is writing a report for school. He's having a little trouble.
Help him by reading the passage and answering the questions below.

I'm writing a report for my health class. It is about important vitamines that our bodies need. I don't think they are as important as my teacher says they are because I can't find information anywhere! I looked up "vitamine" in the dictionary and it is not there. I searched on the Internet for "C" because that is a really important one. The search engine found 4,870,000,000 results! I went through the first 20 pages and there was nothing about vitamines, only Celsius and some programming language.

So then I decided maybe B vitamines are better to look for. I got the B encyclopedia, but there was nothing there either! My report is due next week and I don't know what to do anymore. What am I doing wrong?

1. Why couldn't Roger find what he was looking for in the dictionary? _____

2. What should he search for on the Internet to find out about C vitamins? _____

3. Which encyclopedia should Roger start with? _____

4. List three other places Roger could get information. _____
_____   _____

5. Now that you've told Roger what he should be looking for, try to do the research yourself and see what you can come up with.

_____

_____

_____

_____

_____

_____

On the Blueprint

The Moreno Family is building a new house. Look at the measurements in the blueprint below.

1. The master bedroom is usually bigger than the other bedrooms in a house. Which bedroom would be considered the master bedroom?

_____

2. What is the area of both bedrooms put together?

_____

3. Which is larger, the combined perimeter around the kitchen and the utility room or the perimeter of the garage?

_____

4. Which is smaller, the combined area of the dining room and bedroom #2 or the combined area of the living room?

_____

5. What is the perimeter and area of the whole house and garage?

Perimeter:_____

Area: _____

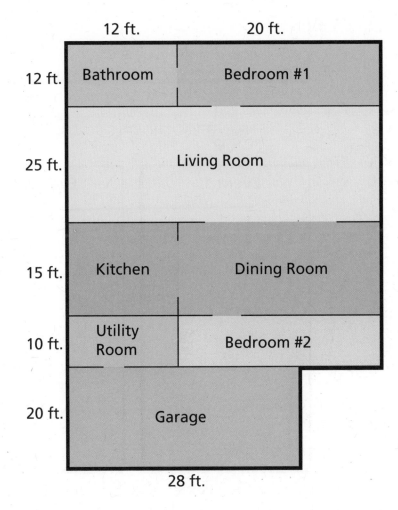

No Problems Here!

Think about a book you've read recently. Use the chart below to map out the main problem of the story and how it is resolved.

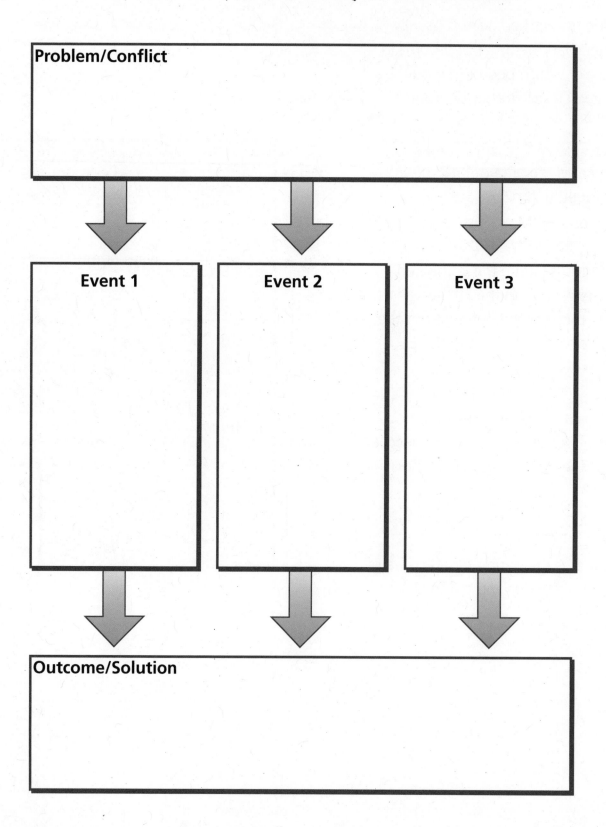

Problem/Conflict

Event 1

Event 2

Event 3

Outcome/Solution

Room to Swim

Matt, Pia, Otto, and Turner each have a fish tank. The fish tanks have different lengths (52 cm, 34 cm, 47 cm, and 51 cm), different widths (2 cm, 15 cm, 11 cm, and 14 cm), and different heights (74 cm, 95 cm, 45 cm, and 61 cm). Use the clues to figure out the length, width, height, and volume for each fish tank.

Clues:

1. The volume of Otto's fish tank is 9,690 cubic centimeters.
2. Pia's fish tank has the smallest height.
3. The length of Pia's fish tank is .34 meters.
4. The volume of Matt's fish tank is 42,328 cubic centimeters.
5. The length of Turner's fish tank is .47 meters.
6. If the length of Pia's fish tank increased by 5 cm, the volume of Pia's fish tank would increase by 3,375 cubic centimeters.
7. Otto's fish tank has the largest height.
8. One fish tank has a width of 11 cm and a height of 74 cm.

	Length				Width				Height				Volume
	34 cm	47 cm	51 cm	52 cm	2 cm	11 cm	14 cm	15 cm	45 cm	61 cm	74 cm	95 cm	
Matt													
Pia													
Otto													
Turner													

What If?

A good way to come up with ideas for a story or report is to ask yourself "What if…" questions, for example, *"What if I won a contest to go to the moon?"* *"What if I lived on a tropical island?"* *"What if the British won the American Revolution?"* Then see where your answers take you.

Think of three "What if…" questions. Write them on the lines. Then think of some possible answers. Don't worry about how crazy or impossible they are! Who knows what kind of great story idea you'll get.

1. What if _____

_____

_____

2. What if _____

_____

_____

3. What if _____

_____

_____

For an extra challenge, take one of your ideas and make it into a story.

Elements Sudoku

Fill in the grid so that every row, every column, and every 3 x 3 box contains one of nine elements.

								Cu
			Ag		Al	Au		Pb
Au	Zn					Al	Ni	
		Ni		Cu			Al	
Cu	Hg			Al	Ag	Fe	Au	
	Au		Zn	Ni		Cu		Ag
Zn							Fe	Au
Fe					Hg			
		Au	Fe					

1. What are the nine elements? _____

_____

2. What do they all have in common? _____

_____

Baby, It's Cold Outside!

Five towns (Horaceville, Ammontown, Miningville, Rowanton, and Laketown) recorded their daily high and low temperatures. The high temperatures were 17°F, –9°F, 22°F, 4°F, and 7°F. The low temperatures were: –4°F, –6°F, –15°F, 6°F, and 8°F.
Use the clues to figure out the high and low temperatures for each town.

Clues:

1. The difference between Miningville's high and low temperature was 11 degrees Fahrenheit.
2. Ammontown's high temperature of the day was 32 degrees Fahrenheit warmer than Horaceville's low temperature of the day.
3. The difference between Rowanton's low temperature and Laketown's high temperature was 28 degrees Fahrenheit.
4. Horaceville had the lowest low temperature of the day.
5. Rowanton's high temperature of the day was warmer than –9 degrees Fahrenheit.
6. Ammontown's low temperature of the day was colder than 8 degrees Fahrenheit.

Ammontown   High: _____   Low: _____

Horaceville   High: _____   Low: _____

Laketown   High: _____   Low: _____

Miningville   High: _____   Low: _____

Rowanton   High: _____   Low: _____

Back-Formations

Back-formations are shortened words created from longer words. Sometimes new words are created by removing affixes from other words. For example, the word *burgle* comes from *burglar*. Here are some back-formations. Can you figure out what word each came from?

1. automate _____

2. aviate _____

3. babysit _____

4. bulldoze _____

5. destruct _____

6. drear _____

7. enthuse _____

8. handwrite _____

9. housekeep _____

10. jell _____

11. sass _____

12. televise _____

Reading Logs

Connor, Hannah, Eliza, Tessa, and Peter read books on Saturday and Sunday. On Saturday they started reading at 8:00 PM, and on Sunday they started reading at 6:30 PM. Their mother kept track of the time they each stopped reading. On Saturday they stopped reading at 9:40 PM, 10:25 PM, 9:50 PM, 11:15 PM, and 9:10 PM. On Sunday they stopped reading at 7:40 PM, 7:10 PM, 7:00 PM, 8:30 PM, and 9:00 PM. Use the clues to figure out how long each person read his or her book on Saturday and Sunday.

Clues:

1. Tessa read a book for two and one-half hours on Sunday.

2. Peter read a book for one and one-third hours longer on Saturday than on Sunday.

3. The person who read one and two-third hours on Saturday was not the one who read two-thirds of an hour on Sunday.

4. Connor read less on Sunday. Connor spent only $\frac{8}{13}$ as much time reading a book on Sunday as she did on Saturday.

5. Eliza read for a total of two and five-sixth hours on Saturday and Sunday.

6. Hannah read a book for two and five-twelfth hours on Saturday.

	Saturday			Sunday		
	Time Started	**Time Stopped**	**Total Minutes**	**Time Started**	**Time Stopped**	**Total Minutes**
Connor						
Eliza						
Hannah						
Peter						
Tessa						

Bonus: Who read for the most total minutes? _____

Shape Equations

The three shapes given all have a different negative value. Each value is a whole number between −10 and −1. Find the value of each shape and then use those values to solve the problems below.

■ × ▲ = 16

● + ▲ = −9

■ < −4

● = −7

■ = _____   ▲ = _____

1. ▲ − ● × ■ ÷ ▲ = _____

2. ● + ▲ + ■ × ■ = _____

3. ● × ■ − ▲ = _____

4. ■ × ● − ● − ▲ = _____

5. ■ ÷ ▲ × ▲ + ● × ■ = _____

6. ■ × ■ − ● + ▲ × ▲ − ■ = _____

Tanka Poems

A *tanka* is an ancient Japanese form of free-verse poetry. Each tanka has five lines. Lines 1 and 3 have five syllables each. Lines 2, 4, and 5 each have seven syllables. Look at the example in the box, then write your own tanka on the subjects below.

> **Friends**
> I love having friends. ⟵ 5 syllables
> They can lift your spirits up. ⟵ 7 syllables
> Friends make you happy. ⟵ 5 syllables
> They are there when you need them. ⟵ 7 syllables
> Where would I be without friends? ⟵ 7 syllables

School
(5 syllables) _____

(7 syllables) _____

(5 syllables) _____

(7 syllables) _____

(7 syllables) _____

Your Favorite Pastime
(5 syllables) _____

(7 syllables) _____

(5 syllables) _____

(7 syllables) _____

(7 syllables) _____

Your Favorite Color
(5 syllables) _____

(7 syllables) _____

(5 syllables) _____

(7 syllables) _____

(7 syllables) _____

Your Summer Vacation

(5 syllables) _____

(7 syllables) _____

(5 syllables) _____

(7 syllables) _____

(7 syllables) _____

Now write tankas on your choice of subjects.

_____(title)

(5 syllables) _____

(7 syllables) _____

(5 syllables) _____

(7 syllables) _____

(7 syllables) _____

_____(title)

(5 syllables) _____

(7 syllables) _____

(5 syllables) _____

(7 syllables) _____

(7 syllables) _____

Persuade Me

Imagine you are trying to convince your parents to get another dog. What reasons would you give? You might say that walking two dogs takes the same amount of time as walking one. You might say the dogs can keep each other company when no one is home. You might say that your dog will be happier with another dog to play with. For each topic below, come up with three persuasive arguments.

1. You want your own computer.

_____

_____

_____

_____

_____

_____

2. You want to go to the beach instead of on a ski vacation this year.

_____

_____

_____

_____

_____

_____

_____

3. You want to go to sleepaway camp.

_____

_____

_____

_____

_____

_____

Women of the American Revolution

Complete the crossword puzzle about famous women and their part in the American Revolution. Use an encyclopedia or the Internet to find answers if you need help.

Across
7. She wrote letters to her husband in the Continental Congress. Much of what she said is in our founding documents. She reminded her husband to take care of the women.

Down
1. She wrote the history of the Revolutionary War: History of the Rise, Progress and Termination of the American Revolution.

2. She was America's first female published African American author. She was a poet, a patriot, and a symbol for those opposed to slavery. She was a slave who was taught to read and write.

3. There may never have been a woman named this, but it was what the women who brought water to the men in battle were called. Once, her husband was wounded in duty. She took over his cannon and fired at the British forces.

4. She has been called the "female Paul Revere." She rode to the nearby villages, warning them of approaching British forces.

5. She is credited with sewing the first American flag.

6. She visited her husband during the war when he was commander-in-chief of the Patriots.

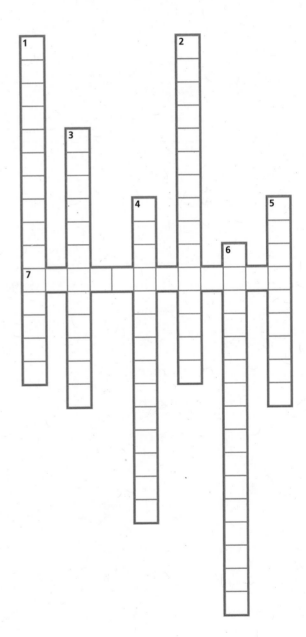

Book Fair

Nena, Pierre, Rebecca, Timothy, and Victor each went to the book fair. At the book fair, they each spent a fraction of the money they brought. They started out with $27, $54, $63, $72, and $90. These fractions of the money were spent: $\frac{1}{9}$, $\frac{2}{9}$, $\frac{5}{9}$, $\frac{7}{9}$, and $\frac{8}{9}$. Use the clues to find how much money each friend spent and how much each had left.

Clues:

1. Whoever started out with $27 has $12 left after the book fair.

2. Rebecca has $12 left after the book fair.

3. Victor has $8 left after the book fair.

4. Whoever started out with $54 has $42 left.

5. Rebecca did not spend $\frac{4}{9}$ of her money.

6. Pierre spent $10.

7. Nena spent more than $\frac{1}{9}$ of her money.

8. Timothy did not spend $\frac{7}{9}$ of his money.

	Starting Money	Fraction Spent	Amount Left
Nena			
Pierre			
Rebecca			
Timothy			
Victor			

170

Summarizing

When you write a summary, you should include only the most important details.
Think about your favorite movie. Write a summary of the movie. Be sure to include the topic,
main idea, the main characters' names, and what events take place.
Add in a few sentences about why other people should go see it.

Movie: _____

Summary: _____

_____

_____

_____

_____

_____

_____

_____

_____

_____

_____

Addison Family Ages

Andrea, Annemarie, Deirdre, Dennis, James, and Joshua Addison are all different ages.
Use the clues to figure out each family member's age.

1. The sum of the ages of Dennis and Annemarie is 78.

2. Annemarie is 34 years older than James.

3. Deirdre's age is 80 less than two times the age of Andrea.

4. In 20 years, Deirdre's age will be 187 less than three times the age of Andrea.

5. Dennis is 12 years younger than Annemarie.

6. In 24 years, Joshua's age will be 134 less than three times his current age.

Person	Age
Andrea	
Annemarie	
Deirdre	
Dennis	
James	
Joshua	

Your Family's Ages

Think about six people in your family. It can be your parents, your sibling, your grandparents, your cousins, or your aunts and uncles. Put the name of each person in the blank chart below. Then, using what you know about each person's age, create six clues to help a friend fill out the chart below. Then give the clues to your friend and see if he or she can find the ages of all six people.

Person	Age

Babbling Babs

Babs has written some word problems for you to solve. Babs likes to babble. She included information that you just don't need to solve the problem. Rewrite the word problem without the unnecessary information. Then solve the problem.

1. It was Friday. Angie got dressed and went to the store. The store was the grocery store. She spent $25.18. The last time she went to the store, she spent only $9.08. But this time she was having a party so she bought lots of snacks. Angie bought 6 cupcakes for her friends. She gave the cashier $30, but she had $50 in her wallet. What was Angie's change?

_____

_____

_____

_____

2. I have a cousin named Paula. Paula loves to ride her bike. She likes to ride on bike paths in the woods. She rode 5.62 miles on Sunday, $4\frac{3}{4}$ miles on Monday, and $\frac{23}{5}$ miles on Tuesday. On Wednesday she was tired. Thursday she had to get her bike fixed at the bike shop, but she drove there. The bike shop is $\frac{9}{5}$ miles from her house. Paula lives $4\frac{1}{2}$ miles from my house. How many miles did she ride her bike this week?

_____

_____

_____

_____

3. Elise gets up at 8:05 AM for camp. She is in the fifth grade. When school is going on, it starts at 9:00. She eats breakfast and brushes her teeth. She had cereal for breakfast yesterday. It takes her 42 minutes to get ready for camp. She leaves when she is ready. Camp starts at 9:30. It gets out at 3:30. What time does Elise leave for camp?

_____

_____

_____

_____

4. Jake took 4 math tests. He got a 90% on the first test, $\frac{24}{50}$ on the second test, 87% on the third test, and $\frac{18}{20}$ on the last test. Last week he got a 95% on his English test. He thinks he got a $\frac{9}{10}$ on his science test. What is the average grade of Jake's math tests as a percent?

_____

_____

_____

_____

5. Kenny, Harris, and Daniel are friends. They like to collect sports cards. Kenny has 3,584 basketball cards and 962 hockey cards. James has 4,278 stamps. Harris has 3,923 baseball cards and 2,895 more basketball cards than Kenny. Daniel has 6,301 football cards and 252 less baseball cards than Harris. How many sports cards do Kenny, Harris, and Daniel have altogether?

_____

_____

_____

_____

6. Out of 80 members of the movie club, 30 voted to watch a comedy next month. 20 voted to watch a drama. 30 voted to watch an action movie. Last month, 50 members voted to watch a romance. The month before that, there were only 75 members. What percent voted to watch a drama next month?

_____

_____

_____

_____

Get the Idea?

Good paragraphs show the main idea in a topic sentence. Then detail sentences connect to each other and to the main idea. Each group of sentences below can be a paragraph from a report. Write *M* for the main idea and *D* for the details.

_____ **1.** Tortillas can be used to scoop up stewed dishes.

_____ **2.** Most Mexican dishes make use of tortillas.

_____ **3.** Enchiladas are tortillas rolled around a filling and have a sauce on top.

_____ **4.** To make tacos, you fold a tortilla in half and fill it with meat, beans, or cheese.

_____ **5.** Its capital is Lima.

_____ **6.** Nearly half of Peruvians are Quechua Indians.

_____ **7.** The people of Peru speak Spanish, Quechua, and Aymara as their official languages.

_____ **8.** Peru is a country in western South America.

_____ **9.** Magma that flows onto the earth's surface is called lava.

_____ **10.** Magma is molten rock that comes from deep within earth.

_____ **11.** When magma cools, it forms igneous rock.

_____ **12.** Magma is usually made of a mixture of liquid, gases, and mineral crystals.

13. Now write your own paragraph with one main idea and three supporting sentences.

_____

_____

_____

_____

_____

_____

_____

_____

_____

_____

Immigration Crossword

Use your knowledge of immigration in the United States to complete this crossword puzzle.

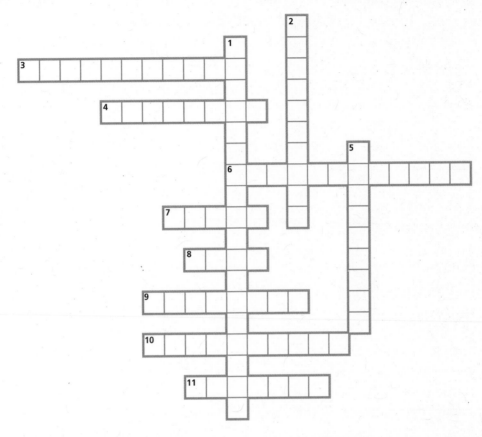

Across

3. A _____ citizen is a person born outside the United States but has U.S. citizens for parents. (2 words)

4. people who flee from their country because their home country is not safe for them

6. _____ immigrants enter the United States without the proper authorization.

7. Any person who is not a citizen or national of the United States is called an _____.

8. This allows a person to apply to come to the United States under a certain classification, like student or temporary worker.

9. to leave one country to live in another

10. A _____ citizen is a person who is granted U.S. citizenship.

11. a person who owes allegiance to the United States and is entitled to its protection

Down

1. people who promised to work for another person for a specified amount of time in exchange for travel and living expenses

2. a _____ citizen is a person born in the United States. (2 words)

5. a person who migrates to another country, usually to live there permanently

One Too Many

The numbers below all have one too many digits. Remove the digit that doesn't belong in order to get a number that is evenly divisible by 3.7. Write the new number that you have made and the answer you get when you divide it by 3.7.

1. 174.8 _____

2. 40.37 _____

3. 151.1 _____

4. 215.9 _____

5. 343.3 _____

6. 48.71 _____

7. 178.5 _____

8. 562.9 _____

9. 1,814.7 _____

10. 2,136.9 _____

Category Catcher

Classify each of the words in the word bank into its proper category below.

asteroid   blizzard   bronchioles   carbon   cilia
colon   comet   diaphragm   galaxy   hail
hurricane   hydrogen   iron   large intestine   lungs
meteor   nitrogen   nose   oxygen   saliva
small intestine   stomach   sun   thunderstorm   tornado

Severe Weather

_____   _____   _____   _____

Solar System

_____   _____   _____   _____

Elements

_____   _____   _____   _____

Digestive System

_____   _____   _____   _____

Respiratory System

_____   _____   _____   _____

Fraction of the Cost

Use information you know about coins to fill in the chart below.

Coin	Decimal Value	Fraction Value
Penny		
Nickel		
Dime		
Quarter		
Half-Dollar		

Now use the chart to write one division equation using decimals and one using fractions to solve each problem below, then solve them.

1. How many nickels are in $0.85? _____   _____

2. How many dimes are in $4.10? _____   _____

3. How many quarters are in $5.75? _____   _____

4. How many half-dollars are in $2.50? _____   _____

Parts of a Book

When you do research for a report, it is important to know where in a book to look for the information you need. Complete the crossword puzzle about parts of a book.

Across

4. This page tells you what year the book was published and who the publishing company is.

5. Look up words you don't know in this part of the book.

6. You can find what page specific topics are on in this part of the book.

Down

1. In this part of a book, you will find titles of other books about the same topic.

2. This page tells you what is in the book.

3. Look on the _____ page for information like who the author is and what the book is called.

How Old Are You Now?

You probably know how old you are in years, but do you know how old you are in months, weeks, days, hours, or minutes? Follow the flow chart below to figure it out. Then try it on a friend or family member.

Step 1. Your age in years + $\dfrac{\text{months since your birthday}}{12}$ = _____

Step 2. _____ $\div \dfrac{1}{12}$ = _____ months old

Step 3. _____ $\div \dfrac{3}{13}$ = about _____ weeks old

Step 4. _____ $\div \dfrac{1}{7}$ = about _____ days old

Step 5. _____ $\div \dfrac{1}{24}$ = about _____ hours old

Step 6. _____ $\div \dfrac{1}{60}$ = about _____ minutes old

Call Me!

Try this math trick for yourself. Then try it on a friend!

1. Write the first three digits of your phone number (without the area code). _____

2. Divide by $\frac{2}{16}$. _____

3. Divide by 0.10. _____

4. Add 1. _____

5. Put 3 zeroes at the end of the number. _____

6. Multiply by 0.25. _____

7. Add in the last four digits of your phone number. _____

8. Add in the last four digits of your phone number again. _____

9. Subtract 250. _____

10. Multiply by 0.5. _____

What do you notice about the number you end up with?

_____

Create a Word Search

You can make your own word search to stump friends and family.

1. First, pick a theme for your word search, like animals or vegetables. _____

2. Now, think of 10 words that fit with your theme.

_____ _____ _____ _____ _____

_____ _____ _____ _____ _____

3. Fill in each of the words in the grid below. Go up, down, backward, forward, diagonal. Have words share letters to make it even more difficult.

4. Fill in the blank boxes with other letters. If you want to stump your friends, make some of the blank spaces parts of the words that you have in there or misspellings of the words.

5. Give your puzzle to friends and see if they can solve it!

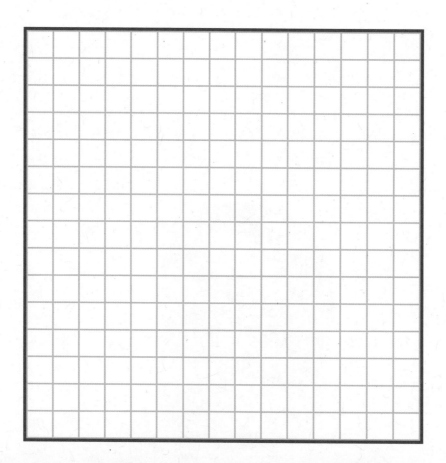

One for the Ages

Follow the steps to learn a new trick you can use on your friends and family.

1. Write down the number of the month you were born. _____

2. Divide by 0.25. _____

3. Add 13. _____

4. Multiply the result by 25. _____

5. Subtract 200. _____

6. Add the day of the month on which you were born. _____

7. Divide by $\frac{2}{4}$. _____

8. Subtract 40. _____

9. Multiply the result by 50. _____

10. Add the last two digits of the year of your birth. _____

11. Finally, subtract 10,500. _____

How does the result compare to your birthday?

_____

Answer Key

Page 4
600,000: 560,431; 612,595; 639,949
700,000: 663,774; 665,043; 709,294; 742,539
800,000: 751,390; 773,016; 801,673

Page 5
Lines should be drawn to match the synonyms as follows:
vague/uncertain; conceal/disguise; monotonous/repetitive; abundant/ample; throng/crowd; deliberate/conscious; sporadic/irregular; accomplished/successful

Page 6
Answers will vary but may include the following:
1. The Middle Colonies were called the "breadbasket colonies" because they grew grains that were used to make bread.
2. The New England Colonies were close to the ocean, which they used for fishing and shipping.
3. The Southern Colonies had few harbors, and their fertile soil made it easy to grow crops.
4. the New England Colonies
5. the Middle Colonies
6. they did not have much coastland.

Page 7

Name	Percentage of fantasy books
Melinda	30.3
Carl	35.9
Adrienne	27.8
Tru	52.9
Debbie	47.8
Joey	43.6
Wendy	42.2
Ramon	19.5
Marco	28.3
Christina	52.1

Page 8
1. admiration
2. optional
3. thanklessness
4. remarkable
5. flexible
6. decrease
7. generous
8. revolutionary

Page 9

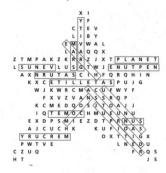

Words in the word search include: Mercury, Saturn, sun Venus, Uranus moon, Earth, Neptune, asteroid Mars, satellite, gravity, Jupiter, planet, comet

Page 10

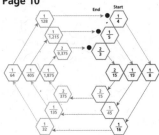

Page 11
Answers will vary but may include the following:
1. nuisance
2. sad
3. be extremely busy
4. wait
5. ready
6. be certain
7. look for
8. together all the time

Page 12
1. Abraham Lincoln
2. Richard Nixon
3. Ronald Reagan
4. George Washington
5. Barack Obama
6. John F. Kennedy
7. Thomas Jefferson
8. Grover Cleveland
9. James Monroe
10. Theodore Roosevelt

Page 13
1. 84°
2. 100°
3. 60°
4. 139°
5. 43°
6. 53°
7. 42°
8. 67°

Page 14
1. 3 hours, 8 minutes
2. 5 hours, 50 minutes
3. 5 hours, 15 minutes
4. 9 hours, 22 minutes
5. 3 hours, 23 minutes

Page 15
"America the Beautiful"
O beautiful for spacious skies,
For amber waves of grain,
For purple mountain majesties
Above the fruited plain!

"I'm a Yankee Doodle Dandy"
I'm a Yankee Doodle Dandy
A Yankee Doodle, do or die
A real live nephew of my uncle Sam
Born on the Fourth of July

"My Country 'Tis of Thee"
My country tis of thee,
Sweet land of liberty,
Of thee I sing.
Land where my fathers died!
Land of the Pilgrim's pride!
From every mountain side,
Let freedom ring!

"This Land Is Your Land"
This land is your land,
This land is my land,
From California
To the New York Island,
From the Redwood forest,
To the Gulf Stream waters,
This land was made for you and me.

Page 16

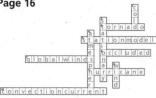

Page 17
1. years
2. inches of snow
3. 2004
4. 2003
5. 2003
6. 2002

Page 18

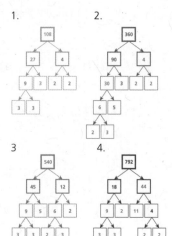

1. [tree diagram: 108; 27, 4; 9, 3, 2, 2; 3, 3]
2. [tree diagram: 360; 90, 4; 30, 3, 2, 2; 6, 5]
3. [tree diagram: 540; 45, 12; 9, 5, 6, 2; 3, 3, 2, 2]
4. [tree diagram: 792; 18, 44; 9, 2, 11, 4; 3, 3, 2, 2]

Page 19
1. capital
2. then
3. stationery
4. than
5. breath
6. affect
7. principal
8. stationary
9. breathe
10. capitol
11. effect
12. principle

Page 20

Name	Number of Pieces in Puzzle	Number of Pieces Put Together of Puzzle	Fraction of Puzzle Completed	Percentage of Puzzle Completed
Lily	55	44	$\frac{4}{5}$	$\frac{4}{5}$ =0.80 .080 X 100= 80%
Omar	132	88	$\frac{2}{3}$	$\frac{2}{3}$ =0.67 .067 X 100= 67%
Olivia	212	159	$\frac{3}{4}$	$\frac{3}{4}$ =0.75 .075 X 100= 75%
Hasid	24	8	$\frac{1}{3}$	$\frac{1}{3}$ =0.33 .033 X 100= 33%
Mary	300	270	$\frac{9}{10}$	$\frac{9}{10}$ =0.90 .090 X 100= 90%
Morgan	82	41	$\frac{1}{2}$	$\frac{1}{2}$ =0.50 .050 X 100= 50%
Irene	91	52	$\frac{4}{7}$	$\frac{4}{7}$ =0.57 .057 X 100= 57%
Terrence	260	104	$\frac{2}{5}$	$\frac{2}{5}$ =0.40 .040 X 100= 40%

Mary won.

Page 21
Answers will vary.

Page 22

Seconds	5	10	15	20	25	30	35	40	45
Miles	1	2	3	4	5	6	7	8	9

Page 23
1. the cat
2. Vincent's cousin
3. the country store
4. Inga's mother
5. Omar
6. Min's vegetable garden
7. the clay sculpture
8. Nina

Page 24
1. lie
2. raise
3. lay
4. set
5. sit
6. rises
7. lie
8. set

Page 25

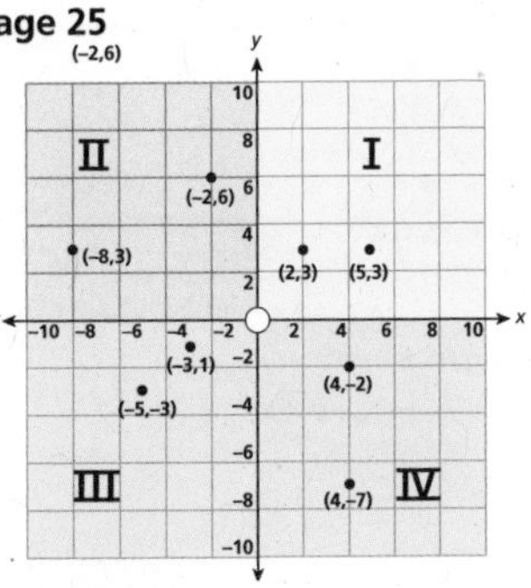

1. quadrant IV
2. quadrant II
3. quadrant I
4. quadrant III
5. quadrant IV
6. quadrant I
7. quadrant III
8. quadrant II

Pages 26–27
1. New Mexico
2. Washington
3. Nebraska
4. Mississippi
5. Minnesota
6. California
7. Colorado
8. North Carolina
9. Oklahoma
10. Montana
11. Florida
12. Massachusetts
13. Oregon and Washington
14. Georgia and Alabama
15. Connecticut and Rhode Island
16. Maine

Page 28
1. simile
2. simile
3. metaphor
4. simile
5. metaphor
6. metaphor
7. metaphor
8. simile
9.–12. Answers will vary.

Page 29
The following should be underlined:
1. walk a million miles
2. waited forever
3. as big as an elephant
4. took me a million years
5. as fast as light
6. I cried for weeks
7. I will die!
8. a billion books
9.–12. Answers will vary.

Page 30
This morning I did not wake up until 7:30. My alarm went off at 7:10, but I was up late last night reading a short story called "Tales of the High Seas." My favorite line in the story was when the captain says, "Walk the plank!" to the prisoner. Then the pirates sang "Life on the Seas." There are three things I like about the story: the way the pirates talk, the adventures they go on, and the interesting places they go. When I get home from school I have to do my homework, do my chores, and eat dinner. Then I will read the story "Mutiny at Midnight." The pirates in that story are: Bluebeard, Pegleg Pete, and One-Eyed Wally.
1. in the time of day and before lists
2. for exact words someone said and for titles of stories and songs
3. before dialogue, between parts in a series, and to separate two complete clauses in a compound sentence

Page 31
It appears to rain inside the jar; Warm, moist air rises to meet the colder air in the atmosphere. Water vapor condenses to form precipitation, like rain, snow, sleet, and hail.

Page 32

Allowance Per Week	A Book Costing $7.50	A CD Costing $9.95	A New Game Costing $14.75	A Pack of New Pencils Costing $2.88	A New Toy Costing $4.99	A New Movie Costing $18.45	A Telescope Costing $27.30	A Calculator Costing $12.20
$1.50	5 weeks	7 weeks	10 weeks	2 weeks	4 weeks	13 weeks	19 weeks	9 weeks
$1.85	5 weeks	6 weeks	8 weeks	2 weeks	3 weeks	10 weeks	15 weeks	7 weeks
$2.25	4 weeks	5 weeks	7 weeks	2 weeks	3 weeks	9 weeks	13 weeks	6 weeks
$3.30	3 weeks	4 weeks	5 weeks	1 week	2 weeks	6 weeks	9 weeks	4 weeks
$3.65	3 weeks	3 weeks	5 weeks	1 week	2 weeks	6 weeks	8 weeks	4 weeks
$4.85	2 weeks	3 weeks	4 weeks	1 week	2 weeks	4 weeks	6 weeks	3 weeks

Page 33
1. autograph
2. transport
3. telegraph
4. teleport
5. import
6. automatic
7. autobiography
8. Answers will vary.

Page 34

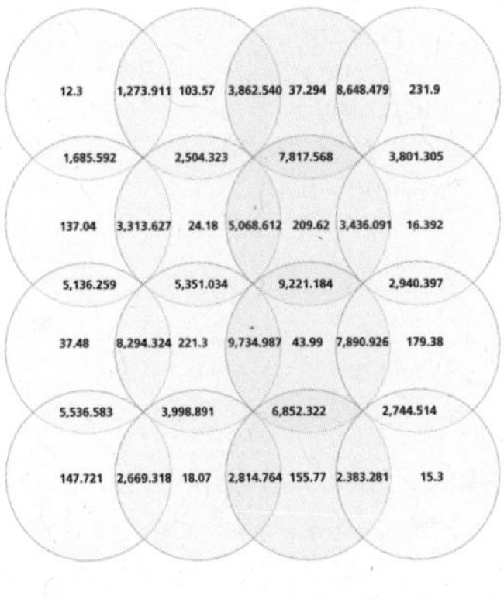

Page 35
1. male, mole, molt
3. wise, wile, file, fill I
2. duel, fuel, feel, kee
4. mild, mile, male, tale
The following matches are correct:
tall/short
skinny/fat
bad/good
old/young
sweet/sour
clean/dirty

Page 36
1. 1.33
2. 2.18
3. 1.39
4. 4.31
5. 7.52
6. 7.1

Page 37
1. pencils, a notebook, crayons, and pens
2. pencils, a pencil sharpener, folders, and pens
3. a notebook, pencil sharpener, folders, and crayons
4. a pencil sharpener, folders, crayons, and pens
5. $1.35
6. $1.60
7. $2.90
8. $1.82
9. 90¢
10. 25¢

Page 38
Answers will vary.

Page 39
1. redder
2. bib
3. sees
4. noon
5. deed
6. peep
7. eye
8. Answers will vary.

Page 40

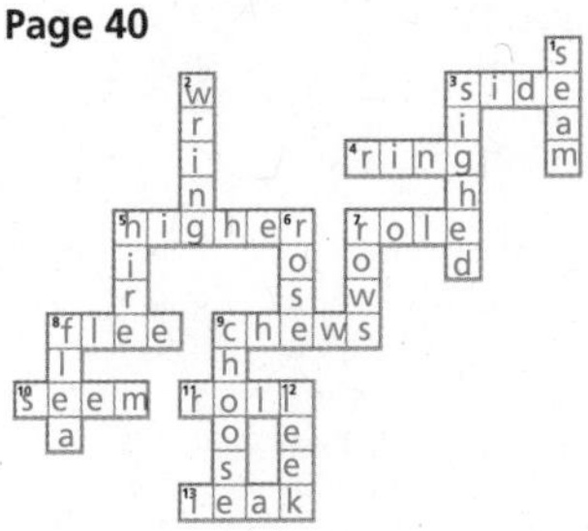

Page 41
Answers will vary.

Page 42
1. correct
2. answer should be 126
3. answer should be -62
4. correct
5. answer should be -79
6. correct
7. correct
8. answer should be -47
9. answer should be -90
10. answer should be -13
11. correct
12. answer should be -26

Page 43
Answers will vary but may include:
1. Water has collected.
2. It came from the leaves.
3. Bigger leaves gave off more moisture.
4. The warmer the leaves get, the more water they lose.
5. The bag is around the leaves so the water could only have come from the leaves.
6. When plant cells break down sugar for energy, they release carbon dioxide and water.

Page 44

Total Miles
$270 \times \frac{2}{3} = 180$ miles (by car) 270 miles (by plane) 270 + 180 = 450 miles (total)
$397 \times \frac{1}{2} = 198.5$ miles (by plane) 397 miles (by car) 397 + 198.5 = 595.5 miles (total)
$180 \times \frac{5}{6} = 150$ miles (by plane) 180 miles (by car) 180 + 150 = 330 miles (total)
$549 \times \frac{2}{7} = 156.9$ miles (by car) 549 miles (by plane) 549 + 156.9 = 705.9 miles (total)
$403 \times \frac{2}{5} = 161.2$ miles (by plane) 403 miles (by car) 403 + 161.2 = 564.2 miles (total)
$730 \times \frac{1}{10} = 73$ miles (by car) 730 miles (by plane) 730 + 73 = 803 miles (total)
$652 \times \frac{3}{8} = 244.5$ miles (by plane) 652 miles (by car) 652 + 244.5 = 896.5 miles (total)
$475 \times \frac{2}{9} = 105.6$ miles (by car) 475 miles (by plane) 475 + 105.6 = 580.6 miles (total)

Grandpa Louis traveled the farthest.

Page 45
1. heart
2. armpit
3. waist
4. finger
5. elbow, bowel
6. dimple
7. palm
8. chin
9.–12. Answers will vary.

Page 46
R = 1/15
H = 6/7
N = 1/3
I = 5/6
Y = 1/6
T = 1/4
E = 10/39
The earth is ninety-three million miles from the sun!

Page 47
Answers will vary.

Pages 48-49

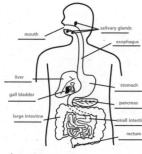

1. pancreas
2. esophagus
3. large intestine
4. rectum
5. mouth
6. salivary glands
7. stomach
8. liver
9. small intestine
10. gallbladder
11. mouth
12. esophagus
13. stomach
14. small intestine
15. large intestine
16. rectum

Page 50

Mean	Median	Mode
87.5	87	93
89.2	89	91
91.2	92.5	94
85.7	85	85

1. Jose
2. Raven
3. 90.9
4. 88

Page 51
Answers will vary.

Page 52
1. Montana
2. Arkansas
3. Alabama
4. Colorado
5. New Hampshire
6. Connecticut
7. Delaware
8. Pennsylvania
9. Texas
10. Utah
11. Michigan
12. Idaho

Page 53
1. $2\frac{4}{5}$
2. 4
3. $3\frac{2}{3}$
4. $3\frac{1}{2}$
5. $4\frac{5}{8}$
6. $6\frac{2}{3}$
7. $8\frac{1}{2}$
8. $5\frac{4}{5}$
9. $9\frac{1}{3}$
10. $14\frac{7}{10}$
11. $6\frac{9}{13}$
12. 4

Page 54
6, 1, 4, 2, 5, 3;
answers will vary

Page 55

G	W	O	N	S	H	X	O	P	V	D	B	S	S	I
G	N	F	U	Y	R	U	D	O	Q	L	M	M	G	V
N	H	I	V	P	X	P	S	B	M	C	I	P	L	F
G	O	E	N	A	C	I	R	R	U	H	D	A	G	X
T	L	X	Q	T	X	L	K	N	M	J	P	W	H	S
N	L	I	H	U	H	N	O	O	S	N	O	M	A	U
O	A	B	I	O	T	G	U	D	Q	B	D	N	N	G
R	U	L	R	P	B	E	I	T	V	P	D	Q	I	D
R	Q	I	E	S	S	M	E	L	X	S	L	O	E	R
E	S	Z	T	R	K	I	I	L	T	B	D	I	N	Z
D	J	Z	S	E	H	E	V	O	S	A	E	C	O	L
N	S	A	I	T	Y	P	R	I	N	C	L	E	L	D
U	X	R	W	A	I	M	E	R	O	N	O	S	C	N
H	A	D	T	W	A	J	O	U	W	S	C	Z	Y	I
T	H	G	R	Q	T	T	M	X	N	E	E	O	C	W

blizzard, ice, sleet, tornado, cyclone, lightning, snow, twister, hail, monsoon, squall, waterspout, hurricane, sandstorm, thunder, wind

Page 56
The correct path has these numbers: 7, 23, 37, 5, 41, 3, 43, 11, 47, 29

Page 57
Sight: glowing, wrinkled, curved; imense
Hearing: boom, buzz, snap, whisper,
Touch: fuzzy, smooth,; warm,; bumpy
Taste: bitter, salty, tangy, ripe
Smell: fishy, musty, damp, fragrant
Answers will vary.

Page 58
1.
  2 small onions
  4 tablespoons olive oil
  4 cups salsa
  6 cups cooked brown rice
  $\frac{1}{2}$ tsp pepper
  1 green bell pepper
  2 pounds chicken legs
  2 pounds spinach
  1 tsp salt
  2 tbsp red pepper flakes
2.
  $1\frac{1}{2}$ small onion
  3 tablespoons olive oil
  3 cups salsa
  $4\frac{1}{2}$ cups cooked brown rice
  $\frac{3}{8}$ tsp pepper
  $\frac{3}{4}$ green bell pepper
  $1\frac{1}{2}$ pound chicken legs
  $1\frac{1}{2}$ pounds spinach
  $\frac{3}{4}$ tsp salt
  $1\frac{1}{2}$ Tbsp red pepper flakes

Page 59
1. feet
2. gallons
3. cubic feet
4. acres
5. square feet
6. cups
7. square inches
8. cubic inches
9. miles
10. inches

Pages 60–61
Answers will vary.

Pages 62–63

Week 1	Week 2	Week 3	Week 4
2.5 lbs	5 lbs	8.75 lbs	11 lbs
1.25 lbs	2.25 lbs	4.25 lbs	6.14 lbs
2.65 lbs	5.07 lbs	9.04 lbs	10.80 lbs
2.25 lbs	4.19 lbs	7.13 lbs	10.44 lbs
2.43 lbs	4.30 lbs	9.65 lbs	10.70 lbs

Week 5	Week 6	Week 7	Week 8
14 lbs	17.5 lbs	21.25 lbs	24.4 lbs
8.22 lbs	10.31 lbs	12.09 lbs	13.22 lbs
13.89 lbs	16.53 lbs	19.40 lbs	22.27 lbs
12.31 lbs	16.5 lbs	19.06 lbs	22.44 lbs
12.63 lbs	16.29 lbs	19.07 lbs	21.15 lbs

1. Janice's
2. Janice's
3. Liu's
4. Liu's
5. Ivan's and Janice's
6. Gregor's
7. Gregor
8. Gregor's and Juan's

Page 64
Answers will vary.

Page 65
Answers will vary.

Pages 66–67

Betty's Variety Store	
Price Per Single Item	Money Made from Packs
$0.95	$41.80
$0.50	$69.86
$0.19	$38.25
$1.33	$32.00
$0.59	$61.75
$0.80	$15.95

Peter's General Store	
Price Per Single Item	Money Made from Packs
$0.90	$37.80
$0.41	$49.50
$0.19	$36.00
$1.00	$40.00
$0.63	$60.64
$0.73	$30.73

1. Betty
2. Betty
3. Peter
4. $14.78
5. Peter
6. Betty

Pages 68–69
Answers will vary.

Page 70
1. 8
2. 64
3. $108
4. 24
5. 21
6. $54
7. $16.50
8. 15

Page 71
Answers will vary.

Page 72
1. fiction
2. fiction
3. nonfiction
4. fiction
5. nonfiction
6. nonfiction
7. fiction
8. nonfiction
9. fiction
10. nonfiction
11. nonfiction
12. fiction

Page 73
1. $24 - 8 = a$
   $a = 16$ hours
2. $365 - 100 = k$
   $k = 265$ days
3. $\frac{1}{4}(40) = s$
   $s = 10$ superhero comics
4. $3(2) = p$
   $p = 6$ pets
5. $3(5) + 4 = c$
   $c = 19$ years old
6. $3(b) - 7 = 38$
   $b = 15$ dollars
7. $6(n + 7) = 192$
   $n = 25$ pounds
8. $5(27) - 13 = d$
   $d = 122$ cards

Page 74
Answers will vary.

Page 75

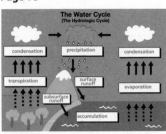

Page 76
1.

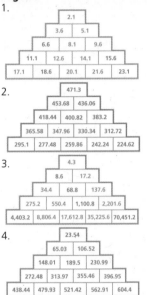

		2.1		
	3.6		5.1	
	6.6	8.1	9.6	
11.1	12.6	14.1	15.6	
17.1	18.6	20.1	21.6	23.1

2.

		471.3		
	453.68		436.06	
	418.44	400.82	383.2	
365.58	347.96	330.34	312.72	
295.1	277.48	259.86	242.24	224.62

3.

		4.3		
	8.6		17.2	
	34.4	68.8	137.6	
275.2	550.4	1,100.8	2,201.6	
4,403.2	8,806.4	17,612.8	35,225.6	70,451.2

4.

		23.54		
	65.03		106.52	
	148.01	189.5	230.99	
272.48	313.97	355.46	396.95	
438.44	479.93	521.42	562.91	604.4

Page 77
1. add 3, add 5
2. add 2, subtract 6
3. subtract 8, add 4
4. subtract 3, add 7
5. add 5, subtract 6
6. 6–10. answers will vary

Page 78
Answers will vary but may include:
1. excellent, exceptional, favorable, great, marvelous, nice, precious, splendid, stupendous, super, wonderful
2. atrocious, awful, cheap, defective, dreadful, garbage, incorrect, inferior, poor, stinking, unacceptable, unsatisfactory
3. appealing, beautiful, charming, cute, darling, delightful, fair, good-looking, handsome, lovely, neat, nice, pleasing
4. brimming, bulky, colossal, enormous, gigantic, huge, immense, jumbo, tremendous, vast

Page 79
1. John Marshall
2. Andrew Jackson
3. Chief Tecumseh
4. James Logan
5. John Ross
6. Sequoyah

Page 80
1. 20.7 – 3.3 = 17.4
2. 37.9 – 10.5 = 27.4
3. 47.25 – 14.87 = 32.38
4. 63.83 – 14.11 = 49.72
5. 71.8 – 19.4 = 52.4
6. 34.21 – 8.53 = 25.68
7. 55.39 – 21.4 = 33.99
8. 91.44 – 26.19 = 65.25
9. 66.9 – 14.22 – 13.32 = 39.36
10. 73.09 – 8.79 – 8.52 = 55.78

Page 81
1. $187
2. $77
3. $176
4. rent
5. insurance and savings
6. $93.50
7. $446.16
8. $77

Pages 82-83

Fact	Opinion
George Washington was born in 1732 and grew up in Virginia.	George Washington is my favorite president.
His mother's name was Mary, and his father was Augustine.	You probably don't know as much about him as I do.
George had three brothers, four half-brothers, and two sisters.	Having sisters is a lot of fun.
When George was young, he liked to explore in the wilderness.	This must have come in handy when he was a general in the Revolutionary War.
He only went to school until he was 14 or 15.	Maybe he was so smart that he didn't need to finish school.
His best subject was math.	His mother must have missed him a lot.
As a teenager, George became a land surveyor.	These are good skills to have.
At 16, he went on an expedition to the western lands for Lord Fairfax.	This was smart for him to do.
It was his first long trip far from home.	I bet he wished he could have traveled overseas more.

Page 84
1. Cherokee
2. Huron
3. Chickasaw
4. Choctaw
5. Seminole
6. Sioux
7. Cheyenne
8. Arapaho
9. Shawnee
10. Iroquois
11. Susquehanna
12. Comanche

Page 85
1. 36 ÷ 9 = 4, 36 ÷ 4 = 9, 4 × 9 = 36, 9 × 4 = 36
2. 25 – 14 = 11, 25 – 11 = 14, 11 + 14 = 25, 14 + 11 = 25
3. 52 ÷ 13 = 4, 52 ÷ 4 = 13, 13 × 4 = 52, 4 × 13 = 52
4. 31 + 12 = 43, 12 + 31 = 43, 43 – 31 = 12, 43 – 12 = 31
5. 63 ÷ 7 = 9, 63 ÷ 9 = 7, 7 × 9 = 63, 9 × 7 = 63
6. 71 – 26 = 45, 71 – 45 = 26, 26 + 45 = 71, 45 + 26 = 71
7. 56 ÷ 7 = 8, 56 ÷ 8 = 7, 7 × 8 = 56, 8 × 7 = 56
8. 41 + 33 = 74, 33 + 41 = 74, 74 – 41 = 33, 74 – 33 = 41
9. 60 ÷ 12 = 5, 60 ÷ 5 = 12, 12 × 5 = 60, 5 × 12 = 60
10. 34 + 49 = 83, 49 + 34 = 83, 83 – 34 = 49, 83 – 49 = 34

Page 86
1. Delaware
2. September 3, 1783
3. 56
4. Q, U, X, Y, and Z
5. Arizona
6. Io, Europa, Ganymede, and Callisto; Jupiter
7. Georgia
8. –273.15°C or –459.67°F

Page 87

Start							
5 ×	90 ÷	8 ×	37 +	14 ×	9 –	50 ÷	1 –
33 +	37 –	20 +	18 ÷	20 +	13 ×	73 +	192 ÷
45 ÷	3 ×	17 –	11 ×	39 +	160 ÷	26 –	0 ×
12 ×	18 +	120 ÷	21 –	2 ×	30 +	14+	63 –
19 –	130 ÷	15 ×	42 –	7 +	18 ×	36 ÷	6 ×
4 ×	7 ×	72 +	90 ×	15 +	4 –	20 ×	60 ÷
64 +	24 –	19 ×	47 +	17 ×	55 +	11 –	29 +
27 ÷	54 +	65 ÷	13 ÷	29 –	25 ×	200 ÷	30 –
							End

Page 88
Komodo Dragon
Lives on Indonesian islands
Between 6 and 10 feet long
Eats animals
Lives in hot, dry places

Both
Can swim
Is a lizard

Australian Water Dragon
Lives in Australia
Between two and three feet long
Eats insects
Lives near water

Page 89
1. Mercury, Mars, Venus, Earth, Uranus, Neptune, Saturn, Jupiter
2. Jupiter, Neptune, Earth, Saturn, Venus, Uranus, Mercury, Mars
3. Saturn, Uranus, Jupiter, Neptune, Mars, Venus, Mercury, Earth
4. Saturn and Jupiter, Uranus, Neptune, Mars, Earth, Venus and Mercury
5. Jupiter, Saturn, Neptune, Uranus, Earth, Mars, Mercury, Venus
6. Jupiter, Saturn, Uranus, Neptune, Earth, Venus, Mars, Mercury

Pages 90
1. population map; A population map shows the population of an area.
2. climate map; A climate map gives information on the long-term weather in an area.
3. relief; A relief map shows shadows to represent the terrain.
4. physical; A physical map shows physical features of the land, such as mountains and different elevations.

Page 91
1. 21.9 – 12.5 = 9.4, 21.9 – 9.4 = 12.5, 12.5 + 9.4 = 21.9, 9.4 + 12.5 = 21.9
2. 6.7 × 8.3 = 55.61, 8.3 × 6.7 = 55.61, 55.61 ÷ 6.7 = 8.3, 55.61 ÷ 8.3 = 6.7
3. 47.28 – 25.68 = 21.6, 47.28 – 21.6 = 25.68, 21.6 + 25.68 = 47.28, 25.68 + 21.6 = 47.28
4. 8.5 × 6.8 = 57.8, 6.8 × 8.5 = 57.8, 57.8 ÷ 6.8 = 8.5, 57.8 ÷ 8.5 = 6.8
5. 42.53 + 18.32 = 60.85, 18.32 + 42.53 = 60.85, 60.85 – 18.32 = 42.53, 60.85 – 42.53 = 18.32
6. 14.29 × 9.3 = 132.897, 9.3 × 14.29 = 132.897, 132.897 ÷ 14.29 = 9.3, 132.897 ÷ 9.3 = 14.29
7. 38.29 + 73.51 = 111.8, 73.51 + 38.29 = 111.8, 111.8 – 38.29 = 73.51, 111.8 – 73.51 = 38.29
8. 5.4 × 7.3 = 39.42, 7.3 × 5.4 = 39.42, 39.42 ÷ 5.4 = 7.3, 39.42 ÷ 7.3 = 5.4
9. 64.2 – 39.47 = 24.73, 64.2 – 24.73 = 39.47, 24.73 + 39.47 = 64.2, 39.47 + 24.73 = 64.2
10. 11.7 × 12.1 = 141.57, 12.1 × 11.7 = 141.57, 141.57 ÷ 12.1 = 11.7, 141.57 ÷ 11.7 = 12.1

Pages 92–93
Mindy won. She marked this row of answers: 29.39; 351.67; 6,041.05; 125.287.

Page 94
1. Answers will vary.
2. Answers will vary.

Page 95
Physical Reaction
crushing a can, sugar dissolving in water, slicing bread, boiling water cutting paper, freezing water Bending a wire, crushing ice crumpling paper, evaporating water in a puddle

Chemical Reaction
iron rusting, eating food, burning wood, fertilizing a garden, souring milk, salting ice on the walkway molding bread, a penny turning green, yeast rising bread, setting off fireworks

Page 96
Answers will vary.

Page 97
1. L
2. C
3. A
4. H
5. B
6. I
7. D
8. J
9. G
10. E
11. K
12. F

Page 98

Answers to questions 1–5 will vary, but may include the following:
1. 12, 24, 36, 48, 60
2. 21, 42, 63, 84, 105
3. 18, 36, 54, 72, 90
4. 10, 20, 30, 40, 50
5. 15, 30, 45, 60, 75
6. 24
7. 21
8. 60
9. 210
10. 315

Page 99

Answers will vary.

Page 100

Crystals (rock candy) should form around the string.

Page 101
1. $10 + 5x$
2. $7y - 56$
3. $60 + 20x$
4. $32y - 72$
5. $18x + 24$
6. $210 - 126y$
7. $140x - 20$
8. $(4x + 28) + (12 - 3x)$
9. $(2y + 16) - (5y - 25)$
10. $(18x + 54) + (52x - 65)$

Page 102

Answers will vary.

Page 103

Answers will vary.

Pages 104–105
1. Ken
2. Walter
3. Henry
4. Suzanne
5. Suzanne
6. Tim
Cards drawn will vary.

Pages 106-107

Answers will vary.

Page 108

Acids: lemon juice, orange juice, grapefruit juice, vinegar, tea
Bases: ammonia, baking soda, soap
Neutral: water, milk, soda

Page 109
1. 2
2. 4
3. 5
4. 8
5. 3
6. 5
7. 3
8. 2
9. 4
10. 7

Pages 110–111

Answers will vary.

Page 112

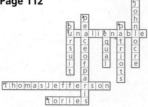

Page 113

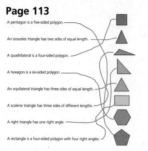

Page 114
1. nucleus
2. proton
3. charge
4. quarks
5. neutron
6. electron
7. molecule
8. negatively

Page 115

Answers will vary.

Page 116

Answers will vary.

Page 117
1. $6 + 3(4) + 7 = 25$ pages
2. $4(2) + 5 + 3(3) = 22$ inches
3. $2 + 3 + 1 - 2 - \frac{1}{4}(2 + 3 + 1 - 2) = 3$ dogs
4. $3(4 + 5 + \frac{1}{3}(4 + 5)) = 36$ years old
5. $3 + 4 + 2(4) + 2(6) = 27$ trees
6. $2(\frac{1}{3}(27) + 3) = 24$ lbs
7. $8 + \frac{1}{2}(8) + 5 - 2(3) + 2 = 13$ people
8. $18 + 2(20) + \frac{1}{2}(18 + 2(20)) + 12 = 99$ cans

Page 118

Page 119

barnyard
bedtime
blacksmith
broadcast
doughnut
foreman
gangplank
hardship
limestone
livestock
nickname
nightmare
photograph
pineapple
starboard
westward

Pages 120-121
1. Penguin
2. Chicken Nuggets
3. Dog and Bear
4. Green
5. Tuna Salad
6. Red
7. Penguin and Dog
8. Brown

Page 122

Answers will vary.

Page 123
1. 50
2. white
3. the 50 states
4. 13
5. 7 red and 6 white
6. the 13 colonies
7. July 4
8. Great Britain
9. George Washington
10. 1787
11. Patrick Henry
12. "The Star-Spangled Banner"

Page 124
1. shortened from *microphone*
2. compound
3. sound
4. sound
5. shortened from *gasoline*
6. borrowed from Spanish
7. name of a character from *A Christmas Carol*
8. blend of *motor* and *hotel*
Challenge: compound of *snow* and *mobile*, and *mobile* is shortened from *automobile*

Page 125

9	3	2	6	5	4	7	1	8
8	5	7	9	2	1	3	4	6
4	1	6	7	3	8	5	2	9
5	2	9	4	1	3	6	8	7
3	7	4	8	6	9	1	5	2
6	8	1	5	7	2	9	3	4
2	6	5	3	8	7	4	9	1
1	4	3	2	9	6	8	7	5
7	9	8	1	4	5	2	6	3

Page 126

Answers will vary.

Page 127

Solids	Liquids	Gases
iron	gasoline	oxygen
wax	alcohol	steam
paper	water	helium
snow	olive oil	
sugar		

Page 128

Answers will vary.

Page 129

8	4	5	1	7	3	9	2	6
6	3	2	4	9	5	8	1	7
9	1	7	8	6	2	3	5	4
1	5	6	2	4	8	7	3	9
2	7	8	3	5	9	4	6	1
4	9	3	7	1	6	5	8	2
3	2	1	9	8	7	6	4	5
7	6	4	5	3	1	2	9	8
5	8	9	6	2	4	1	7	3

Page 130

Western Plains Indians

nomads
followed herds of buffalo
Lakota Indians
carried their belongings on travois

Western Plains Indians

lived in villages
lived in lodges
farmers
Pawnee Indians
Omaha Indians

Both hunted buffalo

Page 131

			16	24	
		23	8	6	9
	3	1	2		17
20	2	7	5	6	
12					
10	8	2		4	4
12	4	8		7	7

Pages 132–133
Old World Monkeys
Found in Africa and Asia
Nostrils close together
32 teeth
Cannot grasp with tail
Some live on the ground
Some have cheek pouches
Opposable thumbs
30 to 100 group members

Both
Primates
Live in groups
Live in trees
Bodies made for moving through trees
Use hands and feet to hold things
Intelligent
Adaptable

New World Monkeys
Found in Central and South America
Nostrils widely spaced out
36 teeth
Some can grasp with tail
Partially opposable thumbs
Less than 20 group members

Page 134
Solid to liquid: melting ice
Liquid to gas: boiling water, humidifier
Solid to gas: dry ice
Gas to liquid: dehumidifier, morning dew, rain
Liquid to solid: cooling magma, freezing water

Page 135
1. Faith, Sun City, Junction, Danville, Mountville, Chaney
2. 306.2 miles
3. 323.7 miles
4. 83.6 miles
5. 641.2 miles

Pages 136-137
Answers will vary.

Page 138
Answers will vary.

Page 139

6	5	**Start 1**	18	17
7	4	2	16	19
8	13	3	15	20
12	9	14	21	23
11	10	**25 End**	24	22

Pages 140–141
1. Rent $5,000
   Utilities $2,000
   Clothing $2,500
   Food $3,000
   Car $2,250
   Medical $1,000
   Taxes $2,500
   Savings $1,250
   Entertainment $2,000
   Miscellaneous $3,500
2. no; $33
3. $500; yes
4. $1,125; $4,625
5. $1,940
6. $625

Page 142
1. deflate
2. underpass
3. not the antonym
4. colorless
5. not the antonym
6. not the antonym
Answers will vary.

Page 143
3, 5, 8, 6, 7, 4, 1, 2

Page 144
1. *aud*
2. *vid, vis*
3. *port*
4. *spec, spic, scope*
5. *struct*
6. *man*
7. *ject*
8. *ped*
9. *bibl*
10. *fin*
11. *meter*
12. *photo*

Page 145
Lunch and dinner.

Page 146
Philadelphia has been called the birthplace of the United States. Neither the Declaration of Independence and the U.S. Constitution were signed there. Philadelphia also served as the capital of the American colonies from 1776 to 1782.

Philadelphia was founded by William Penn in 1582. Penn was a French Quaker who was persecuted for his beliefs. Because of this, Penn never wanted Philadelphia to be a place of religious freedom. Philadelphia's nickname is "The City of Brotherly Love" because pennsylvania means *brotherly love* in Latin. American Quakers still have their headquarters there.

In 1790, there were about 42,000 people living in Philadelphia, making it the second largest city in the nation. Today the city's population is about 1.5 million. It is the largest city in Pennsylvania.

Page 147
1. 16
2. 31
3. 11, 22, 33, 44
4. 13, 26, 39
5. 3, 5, 7, 9
6. 42
7. 24, 25, 26, 27, 28 and 32, 33, 34, 35, 36
8. 30 and 42

Page 148
These sentences should be crossed off:
1. My mother says that I make mountains out of molehills. I'm afraid of heights.
2. My cousin is allergic to tomatoes. The ocean has lots of salty water. We learned about acids in science class.
3. Do you remember that cricket from *Pinocchio*? He wore clothes. In my family, my mother is the best singer. I don't like to get lost.
4. My parents like to have dinner by candlelight. I like blowing out the candles on my birthday cake. My hobby is stamp collecting.

Page 149

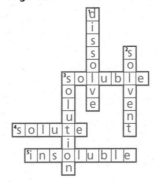

Page 150
1. 16
2. 3
3. 6
4. 2
5. $\frac{1}{3}$
6. 3
7. 16
8. 6

Page 151

Fraction	Decimal
½ dollar per can	0.50 dollar per can
2/3 dollar per loaf	0.67 dollar per loaf
¾ dollar per box	0.75 dollar per box
3/5 dollar per bag	0.60 dollar per bag
1/3 dollar per can	0.33 dollar per can
5/6 dollar per bottle	0.83 dollar per bottle
4/5 dollar per orange	0.80 dollar per orange
3/7 dollar per bag	0.43 dollar per bag

Pages 152-153

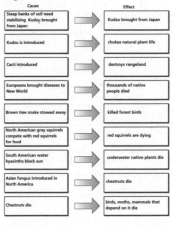
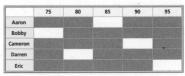

Page 154

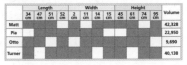

Page 155
1. 21
2. 13
3. 6
4. 15

Page 156
1. He spelled vitamin wrong.
2. He should search for "vitamin C."
3. He should get the V volume for vitamin.
4. Answers will vary.
5. Answers will vary.

Page 157
1. bedroom #1
2. 440 square feet
3. garage
4. dining room and bedroom #2
5. Perimeter: 228 feet; Area: 2, 544 square feet

Page 158
Answers will vary.

Page 159

	Length				Width				Height				Volume
	34 cm	47 cm	51 cm	52 cm	2 cm	11 cm	14 cm	15 cm	45 cm	61 cm	74 cm	95 cm	
Matt													42,328
Pia													22,950
Otto													9,690
Turner													40,138

Page 160
Answers will vary.

Page 161

Al	Pb	Fe	Ni	Au	Zn	Hg	Ag	Cu
Hg	Ni	Cu	Ag	Fe	Al	Au	Zn	Pb
Au	Zn	Ag	Cu	Hg	Pb	Al	Ni	Fe
Ag	Fe	Ni	Hg	Cu	An	Pb	Al	Zn
Cu	Hg	Zn	Pb	Al	Ag	Fe	Au	Ni
Pb	Au	Al	Zn	Ni	Fe	Cu	Hg	Ag
Zn	Cu	Hg	Al	Pb	Ni	Ag	Fe	Au
Fe	Ag	Pb	Au	Zn	Hg	Ni	Cu	Al
Ni	Al	Au	Fe	Ag	Cu	Zn	Pb	Hg

1. Au = Gold, Ag = Silver, Cu = Copper, ZN = Zinc, Al = Aluminum, Pb = Lead, Hg = Mercury, Ni = Nickel, and Fe = Iron
2. They are all metals.

Page 162

Ammontown High: 17 Low: 6
Horaceville High: −9 Low: −15
Laketown High: 22 Low: 8
Miningville High: 7 Low: −4
Rowanton High: 4 Low: −6

Page 163

1. automation
2. aviation
3. babysitter
4. bulldozer
5. destruction
6. dreary
7. enthusiasm
8. handwriting
9. housekeeper
10. jelly
11. sassy
12. television

Page 164

	Saturday			Sunday		
	Time Started	Time Stopped	Total Minutes	Time Started	Time Stopped	Total Minutes
Connor	8:00	11:15	195	6:30	8:30	120
Eliza	8:00	9:40	100	6:30	7:40	70
Hannah	8:00	10:25	145	6:30	7:10	40
Peter	8:00	9:50	110	6:30	7:00	30
Tessa	8:00	9:10	70	6:30	9:00	150

Page 165

■ −8
▲ −2
1. 26
2. 55
3. 58
4. 65
5. 48
6. 82

Pages 166–167

Answers will vary.

Page 168

Answers will vary.

Page 169

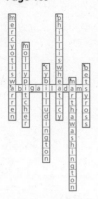

Page 170

	Starting Money	Fraction Spent	Amount Left
Nena	$63	$\frac{7}{9}$	$14
Pierre	$90	$\frac{1}{9}$	$80
Rebecca	$27	$\frac{5}{9}$	$12
Timothy	$54	$\frac{2}{9}$	$42
Victor	$72	$\frac{8}{9}$	$8

Page 171

Answers will vary.

Page 172

Person	Age
Andrea	65
Annemarie	45
Deirdre	54
Dennis	33
James	11
Joshua	79

Page 173

Answers will vary.

Pages 174-175

1. Angie spent $25.18. She gave the cashier $30. What was Angie's change? $4.82
2. Paula loves to ride her bike. She rode 5.62 miles on Sunday, $4\frac{3}{4}$ miles on Monday, and $2\frac{3}{5}$ miles on Tuesday. How many miles did she ride her bike this week? 14.97 miles
3. Elise gets up at 8:05 a.m. for camp. It takes her 42 minutes to get ready for camp. She leaves when she is ready. What time does Elise leave for camp? 8:47 A.M.
4. Jake took 4 math tests. He got a 90% on the first test, $\frac{24}{50}$ on the second test, 87% on the third test, and $\frac{18}{20}$ on the last test. What is the average grade of Jake's math tests as a percent? 78.75%
5. Kenny, Harris, and Daniel like to collect sports cards. Kenny has 3,584 basketball cards and 962 hockey cards. Harris has 3,923 baseball cards and 2,895 more basketball cards than Kenny. Daniel has 6,301 football cards and 252 less baseball cards than Harris. How many sports cards do they have altogether? 24,920
6. Out of 80 members of the movie club, 20 voted to watch a drama. What percent voted to watch a drama next month? 25%

Page 176

1. D
2. M
3. D
4. D
5. D
6. D
7. D
8. M
9. D
10. M
11. D
12. D
13. Paragraphs will vary.

Page 177

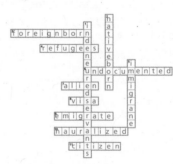

Page 178

1. 14.8; 4
2. 40.7; 11
3. 11.1; 3
4. 25.9; 7
5. 33.3; 9
6. 48.1; 13
7. 18.5; 5
8. 62.9; 17
9. 114.7; 31
10. 136.9; 37

Page 179

Severe Weather: tornado, hurricane, thunderstorm, hail, blizzard
Solar System: comet, galaxy, asteroid, meteor, sun
Elements: oxygen, nitrogen, hydrogen, carbon, iron
Digestive System: saliva, stomach, small intestine, large intestine, colon
Respiratory System: lungs, nose, diaphragm, bronchioles, cili

Page 180

Coin	Decimal Value	Fraction Value
Penny	0.01	$\frac{1}{100}$
Nickel	0.05	$\frac{1}{20}$
Dime	0.10	$\frac{1}{10}$
Quarter	0.25	$\frac{1}{4}$
Half-Dollar	0.50	$\frac{1}{2}$

1. $0.85 \div 0.05 = 17$ or $\frac{85}{100} \div \frac{1}{20} = 17$
2. $4.10 \div 0.10 = 41$ or $4\frac{1}{10} \div \frac{1}{10} = 41$
3. $5.75 \div 0.25 = 23$ or $2\frac{3}{4} \div \frac{1}{4} = 23$
4. $2.50 \div 0.50 = 5$ or $\frac{5}{2} \div \frac{1}{2} = 5$

Page 181

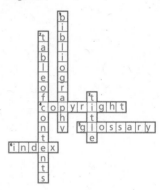

Page 182

Answers will vary. Here are some examples of correct answers:
1. $11\frac{6}{12}$
2. 138 months
3. 598 weeks
4. 4,186 days
5. 100,464 hours
6. 6,027,840 minutes

Page 183

You should end up with your phone number!

Page 184

Answers will vary.

Page 185

The number should be your birth month, day, and last two digits of the year you were born! For example, if your birthday is October 12, 1999, the number you would get is 101299.